Also by Chris Griscom:

Time Is an Illusion
Ecstasy Is a New Frequency
Nizhoni: The Higher Self in Education
Ocean Born: Birth as Initiation

THE HEALING OF EMOTION

Awakening the Fearless Self

CHRIS GRISCOM

A FIRESIDE BOOK
PUBLISHED BY SIMON & SCHUSTER INC.

New York   London   Toronto
Sydney   Tokyo   Singapore

Fireside
Simon & Schuster Building
Rockefeller Center
1230 Avenue of the Americas
New York, New York 10020

Originally published in the Federal Republic of
Germany by Wilhelm Goldmann Verlag.
Original German edition by Chris Griscom with
Wulfing von Rohr
FIRESIDE and colophon are registered trademarks
of Simon & Schuster Inc.

DESIGNED BY BARBARA MARKS GRAPHIC DESIGN
Manufactured in the United States of America

10 9 8 7 6 5 4 3 2 1

Library of Congress Cataloging in Publication Data
Griscom, Chris
    The healing of emotion: awakening the fearless
self / Chris Griscom.
        p.   cm.
    "A Fireside book."
    1. Self-actualization (Psychology)
2. Emotions.   3. New Age movement.   I. Title.
BF637.S4G77   1990   89-78066
152.4—dc20   CIP

ISBN 0-671-68635-6

Acknowledgments

*I dedicate
this book
to my family:
Leonard, Kay,
Kathy, Betty,
Alex, Karin,
David, Britt,
Megan, Teo,
Bapu, Dakotah,
and Luke.*

My admiration and gratitude to Barbara Gess, my editor, for her clear expertise and support of this work.

Elizabeth Petofi, the unseen saint and champion of this book, who bent time in a hundred ways to prepare this manuscript on schedule, supporting and encouraging me to complete it—thank you, thank you, Elizabeth.

Pat Martin, who trekked through the New Mexican sun to take the cover photo of me in one of my sacred energy spots—thank you.

Many, many thanks to Dennis Kucinich for reading the manuscript and so skillfully contributing to the editing process.

CONTENTS

A Word to the Reader

Fear is with us all our life. It is the ultimate source of unhappiness, disease, and war. Even as our embryonic bodies are forming in our mother's womb, we begin to absorb the energy of fear through the psychic matrix of emotional patterns called the emotional body. Just as we have a physical pattern of DNA that sets up the blueprint of our physical body, we have an emotional DNA that rides piggyback and carries into the body a prearranged framework of emotional characteristics that become activated by the spiritual and psychic channels we share with our parents.

Emotional experiences radiate throughout the biochemical nervous system of the mother and are also imposed upon the fetus, which has no filter that can discriminate between good and bad substances or energies coming its way. The fetus simply takes in everything in its environment, for better and for worse.

Our divine soul selects parents whose emotional patterns fit the needs of our own emotional body, in terms of influencing the quality and kinds of emotional experiences we need in order to grow spiritually. From the moment of conception to our death, we are vulnerable and open to our parental emotional patterns, as well as to the ones we develop throughout our lives.

Thus we come into the world with an emotional repertoire already intact. From a spiritual perspective, the emotional body is composed of imprints that have been experienced in many dimensions and many incarnations of the soul's journey to enlightenment. Since the emotional body is an entity of consciousness that thrives on energies outside of time and space, it is already disposed to seek out and repeat the emotions it can recognize and perceive.

From the point of pure consciousness, we have all chosen to return again and again to the body for the purpose of the enlightenment of our soul. Each time, however, the actual experience of separating from that formless universal level, and crossing the threshold into the limitation of bodily form, creates a profound anxiety that veils the point of access so that there is a clouding of the memory and we suffer an insurmountable fear whose source we cannot remember.

This book, *The Healing of Emotion,* will lead us safely through the pitfalls of our lapse of memory, through the patterns and habits of our primordial emotional bodies, back to that pinhole in the cosmic sky from which we emerged. As we learn to discover the nuances of the emotional body, we will discover how easily we can regain balance in our lives and . . . Awaken the Fearless Self!

Thus, the healing tool turns out to be consciousness itself, the very goal of incarnation. Consciousness does not come about in a linear, logically conclusive, and traceable course of events, but rather as a spiral evolution. We attain new dimensions of consciousness more by associative awareness, rather than by rational analysis. In circular movements, we return to former points of departure and problem sources, albeit on an ever higher octave.

The central message of this book is that only spiritual energies, only the spiritual light, can heal us, and that we can easily learn to call this spiritual energy into ourselves through our consciousness. Our goal is not something that is separate from us. It is not a religion or ideology or anything that is not a part of everyday life. Our Higher Self is always here. The divine light and spiritual energy are also always here. We can not only experience them within and by ourselves, we *are* these energies! Naturally, this is nothing new. And naturally, we seek help from outside time and again.

I founded both the Light Institute and the Nizhoni School for Global Consciousness to create a structured environment for those seeking the Higher Self. I designed our work to give people the actual tools of consciousness with which they can truly access their own inner knowing and thus be able to comprehend and instruct the currents of their lives.

This book is conceived as a holographic experience that invites you to read it with your whole being, with intelligence, heart, and soul. The multitudinous threads are picked up and rewoven with one another in order to allow a widening arch of recognition so that, as we find ourselves mirrored in emotional dilemmas, we also begin to see a reflection of light that frees us to explore further. Adventure and wonderment are the magnificent rewards of the Fearless Self!

Chris Griscom
Galisteo, New Mexico, August 1989

1

The Separation Trauma

Our lives seem filled with separations, schisms, leavetaking. We take leave of someone, we terminate a relationship, there is a death. We separate after lovemaking. We divorce. Children leave the house. The infant stops suckling at its mother's breast. At birth, we separate—or are separated—from the protective shield of our mother. And to go back even farther: at some point, somehow, our spirits, our divine spark, separated from God.

We have emerged from the formless. The soul has decided to become incarnate. Thus we create the body that is to become our new home of existence. It is a "young" expression, which means the externalization of the source energy that moves toward our manifestation. By means of the yang energy, we surge outward from creation, and then suddenly find ourselves in a body and in a new environment. The door behind us gradually closes, the connection to the creative source, to our divine self, becomes nebulous as our consciousness narrows down into the realm of the physical. Unacknowledged by the world of form, the divine self retires into the formless—and thus our fear begins.

We know that we want to acquire form. Our souls have made this decision. With our own creative powers we execute a conscious act, that of incarnation. But as soon as this act is executed, and the concomitant separation takes place (the body is the separation), doubts crop up, as do fear and anger, because direct recognition of this choice and knowledge dissolve. Our memory of the conscious decision to become incarnate disappears, and for the first time, the body has to orient itself outward to seek survival. Thereby, it begins to experience fear and anger and anguish about the separation. Deeply imbedded in the blueprint of embodiment is this memory of oneness, the universal mergence of all life.

Every separation enhances our desire to regain the lost connection with an essence we don't consciously remember. With every new separation, we experience different aspects of our vital dilemma: to be cut off, isolated, divorced from an overall, embracing life context, to be isolated within a limited consciousness. No matter how often we may have chosen these separations ourselves, perhaps in order to progress in our individualization, the actual separations of consciousness nonetheless keep triggering an impulse to regain the lost wholeness.

Typically, two basic archetypal emotions, fear and anger, characterize these cyclical separation processes. Fear and anger are two different manifestations of one single, fundamental reaction on the part of the emotional body. They are the two core emotions that express the separation trauma—whether it is one of the big, original separations such as the separation from God or the separation at birth, or whether it is but one of the everyday separations.

As we consider the "hologram," the totality of our experiences, we see that birth or some other profound process of separation sets a kind of energy in motion. In the course of our further experiences, this energetic motion leads us back to the point of departure in a circular way. The separation or isolation or divorce cannot completely cover up our memory of what is real. The limitations and obstacles we experience in our "new identity" as isolated beings—at the same time as we are experiencing new possibilities and challenges—evoke fear and anger.

In this book we will explore the fundamental aspects of fear and anger and investigate the ways and means of overcoming them. Fear is the "feminine," the "yin" way of experiencing our hurt of separation. Fear is that yin energy that often finds its manifestation in defense, rejection, and resistance against someone or something. Fear is a form of energy that literally drowns the vital forces and is far more dangerous than anger. For while anger keeps the organism in motion and lends the organism vital forces (albeit possible destructive forces), anxiety and fear swallow up and gnaw at the organism.

Anger represents the "male," the "yang" way of expressing our pain of changing dimensions. We are human beings who possess a multifaceted consciousness, we are "multidimensional" beings. In the final analysis, we are consciousness! Hidden within us lies a primarily buried treasure of knowledge, of love, happiness, strength, and life! As we acquire the limitations of a body, coming from this almost magical omnipotence and omniscience, as we gain a "human" perspective through our terrestrial incarnation, as we incarnate ourselves in the standard dimensions of time and space, we leave the main part of our holographic, multidimensional consciousness behind us. We emerge as limited, separate beings, as individuals; we separate ourselves from the direct, immediate experiencing that is all-pervasive being.

Initially after birth, we are still open for psychic, spiritual experiences. But as time passes, we forget more and more how to talk with fairies, elves, angels, and other forms of consciousness. We are governed to an ever greater extent by the adult world with its analogous, linear way of thinking. Fear and anger become our companions more and more consciously. We are afraid not to be able to cope with life. We are afraid of snakes, spiders, and rats, or afraid of flying. We are afraid of our parents or siblings or friends. We are afraid of punishment or violence. We are afraid we will not have enough to eat, afraid to descend into the dark cellar, of getting lost in the forest; afraid that this or that person does not love us, that we will be rejected by him or her. The fears are without number; and, as we know, they exist not only on the level of waking consciousness but also within our subconscious. Often our dreams reflect even worse fears than those experienced during the daytime.

Just as we are not conscious of the reasons we experience fear, at least not in the first months, years, or even decades of our lives, we also frequently find ourselves or others being angry without reason. We know the temper tantrums, the rage, of children, adolescents, and even of adults who want to impose their will on others with all their might. We know that we are capable of crying from sheer anger. We know the rage at "life" or "the world" or perhaps at "the others" for not conforming to our images of them, for not fulfilling our wishes.

One could say that fear arises because we feel incapable of getting involved with life, of accepting life and embracing it. Anger, on the other hand, arises when we feel unable to express and live all of who and what we truly are.

All of us have squeezed our divine energy into a specific form. We have, in truth, caged it therein, and now we seem unable to liberate ourselves from this form we have chosen. As a result of the separation from universal consciousness at birth, fear and anger become powerful impulses that impel us over and over again to regain our original, holographic being by striving to return to that celestial womb that we sense is our MOTHER, our source.

The difficulty of coming into body (incarnating in physical form) is that we are exposed to an entirely different set of energy laws that govern consciousness. In the realm of the formless, there is no filter that interrupts the endless stream of pure consciousness. On the contrary, our physical world forces consciousness through the sieve of the perceptual modality in which cognition describes, weighs, and measures every particle of awareness in such a way that the vast interweaving latticework of holographic reality is lost. Our perceptual or sensory reality is attached to the biochemistry of our physiological system from which stems the emotional body.

❧   *The Emotional Body*   ❧

We are not just one concrete physical organism. We are a dynamic, living tapestry of several bodies woven together in such a way as to facilitate an integration of very complex deductive, sensory, and experiential realities. These are the physical, mental, spiritual, and emotional bodies.

The emotional body is paramount among the bodies because of its overpowering influence upon our view of the world and ourselves in it. It is literally an entity of consciousness who lives, for the most part, an obsessive, destructive, yet hidden existence within the unexplored reaches of the subconscious void. The dislocated emotional body is the epitome of our separation from all that is divine, universal God. Yet we must look within the mirror of the emotional body to know the truth of our illusions, so that we can clear away the debris and the sludge and return untarnished to the pure, liquid light of our true selves.

The emotional body represents an aspect of ourselves that is not subject to time and space. If we lose our physical body, our emotional body remains whole nonetheless and merely seeks to connect with a genetic code, the DNA of a new body in a new lifetime, which we then inhabit and through which the emotional body can continue to operate. The "old" emotional body brings all those perceptions, experiences, reaction patterns, and conceptions of reality that it has acquired in our other incarnate bodies, in other times, with it into the "new" physical body. Thus it is not subject to the one-dimensional illusion of the time and space of one life.

Sadly, the repertoire of the emotional body is bound by imprints that are mostly slow and dense in nature. These are the frequencies of anger, fear, remorse, negativity. In fact, the higher, faster vibrations of ecstatic emotions such as love, bliss, and rapture are almost too fleeting to be recorded in the astral energies associated with form. We have come to identify ourselves with our emotions, which are only the outer crust of the actual emotional body that interfaces and feeds the body through its experiential emotional repertoire.

The emotional body controls our existence on this planet on all levels of consciousness. Although the mind is able to alter and even transform the physical body, it has little more than a superficial effect on the powerful emotional body. Thus we can command our emotional body with our mind—"I don't want to be angry anymore"—and still experience the insidiousness of anger within. Obviously we can cover up the anger with the aid of affected behavioral patterns so that it is not visible to the outside world, so that we are not completely dominated by the anger. But always when we repress it by control mechanisms, it will break through at some other time, in some other place, in some other way. One way is in the form of illness.

✔   *Anger and Separation*   ➘

The pain of separation from our source, separation from God, leaving the womb, divorcing a formerly beloved partner, always means—unless we have cleared the emotional body—that those forms of energy that are fear and anger have crystallized within us as determinants of our emotional bodies. These hardened, pent-up energies keep causing reactions, psychic and physical repressions, and a feeling of personal inadequacy and unhappiness.

Rage, anger, and fury are all explosive kinds of energy, a yang kind of energy that needs to be expressed outwardly. Anger is a defense mechanism, a technique for survival. At the same time, anger is felt as being a vital energy, almost as though one were saying, "I feel anger, thus I am alive." When the angry energy shoots up within us, we feel compelled to express it, as, otherwise, we feel we would die. However, anger can be very useful because it moves us, thrusts us, into action. We can use the power of anger as an impulse to progress farther along our spiritual path. We can also use the energy of anger on an emotional level of expression and even as an energizing force on a physical level. If we could grasp within our consciousness that the source of all anger comes from the illusion of separation from our spiritual spring, we could dissolve it forever.

If we reflect carefully and take a close look at ourselves, we will notice that, initially, anger covers up fear. The first emotion we experience after a painful separation is fear, and then comes anger as a reaction to the profound fear. We are afraid to continue life alone, after the death of our parents, say, or after our partner has left us. We are angry at those persons who appear to have deserted us. If we consciously experience how anger builds up, then explodes, and, finally, after the smoke has dissipated, clears the view so that we can see the cause of our anger, we invariably find a fearful human being, a quaking child, an anxious and limited consciousness caught up in some memory of the emotional body.

To want to survive expresses a very positive energy, with a goal—to fight, to deal with the adverse circumstances of life. Our profound anger at those forces serves as a powerful stimulant to change precisely those circumstances. Thus far, then, anger is a constructive transformation of fear. However, like the proverbial rabbit when it encounters a snake, as long as we remain caught up in fear in a purely receptive and passive manner, we destroy our own life force, often so gradually and slowly that we do not perceive it.

With every separation, every isolation or exclusion from some larger communion, we suffer the experience of limiting our consciousness. We "forget" our divine origin. We "forget" our encompassing freedom, our ability to survive any and all circumstances. We "forget" that we constantly enter voluntarily into new learning situations, such as physical incarnation—to attain a single goal: to close the circle again, to return to the starting point of our journey through universes, dimensions of consciousness, and life forms with ever-increasing consciousness until at last we recognize that we penetrate creation, genius. The God Force grows and expands through us!

We "forget" our perfection, our all-encompassing spiritual being. This is a fantastic, cosmic joke; in fact, the joke is on us. We detach a part of our consciousness from the whole, force the spiritual spark into three-dimensional garb, slip and slide into the illusion of time construed by ourselves, and negate our grandiose divine origin and all concomitant powers of manifestation.

The voluntary separation and incarnation of a part of our consciousness into the physical body is conducive to the growth of our souls, to the realization of the divine power into life forms, into manifestation. With this separation we detach ourselves, we take leave of one dimension in order to experience another, and thus we initially experience loneliness, emptiness, insecurity, and mourning. As long as we are determined by these feelings, we will not be capable of merging with another person to such a degree that a symbiotic relationship can emerge. The longing to merge completely with another out of loneliness almost always leads to the energy merely flowing from one partner to the other and not to a true mutual exchange on a similar or compatible plane of energy.

As long as we believe we need another person (or thing, cause, organization, mission, or task) in order to become whole ourselves, we will inevitably keep getting lost in ghost towns of feelings, thoughts, and projections. We then count on the outside world, on having forces other than our own, abilities and authorities outside ourselves, to help us survive, grow, and become fulfilled. Thereby we give ourselves away—and end up empty-handed.

Until we experience that the whole universe exists within us, that we are always and forever connected to everything that is, both the manifest and unmanifest world, we will not be able to join the cosmic giggle and find peace in our lives. Our fear of being alone, as a consequence of the thrust into life at conception, has led us to a tragic misconception—that we must fight to survive. If we succeed in awakening universal consciousness, we will know unequivocally that survival is the divine plan of the cosmos; energy is never lost, it simply transmutes and reshapes itself to contribute to the magnificent dance of evolution. We, ourselves, are the stars of evolution!

Let us now discover the luminous, unmanifested source of consciousness that is omnipresent. In some mysterious way, it fills us with the waters of life, with love for ourselves and for all forms of living energy that surround us. As we experience this earthly existence, we are like the proverbial rubber band, stretched so tautly that it threatens to snap, just as the surge of energy reaches the critical point that is strong enough to hurl it, via the force that pulls it apart, back to the central point from which it first emerged.

✔   *Anxiety: The Usurper of Energy*   ❧

Anxiety is even more dangerous to us than anger, because anxiety causes a dispersal, a loss, of energy; in a fit of rage, however, we come from our center, almost literally throwing ourselves outward. A fairly frequent characteristic of anxiety is that our center disappears; we can no longer find it. An additional factor is that we very rarely know what caused the anxiety initially.

There is a palpable difference between fear and anxiety, as well. Anxiety is a rather diffuse, indeterminate feeling, while fear relates more to a concrete situation or object. We know fear of death, fear of separation. They are things or situations outside us, while anxiety lurks around in the nebulous corners of our mind, inside the nervous system, tucked away inside the disoriented self. Especially in depressed states, relatively tangible fear themes blend into a general anxiety. Anxiety disrupts the ability to find the self or the center and, therefore, the ability to attain knowledge.

In our physical body we generally carry our anxiety across the breadth of our chest. This is the reason so many people have respiratory problems and also why people smoke. Everything that partially or wholly blocks our breathing, such as smoking, sources or enhances anxiety. A sure sign of anxiety is tension in the shoulders, steered by the deltoid muscle. Anxiety is expressed visually when we cross our arms over our chest or solar plexus.

By doing this we try to protect ourselves emotionally from some threat. This starts when we receive vibrations from our surroundings via the solar plexus at a very young age.

When the vibrations around us are negative, as a result of anger, self-righteousness, or anxiety, we as children automatically become tense in the solar plexus chakra because the emotional body is imprinted by outside vibrations through this center. The tension is a result of the fact that those vibrations do not correspond to the child's naturally higher vibrations. That which normally evokes a fight-or-flight response is absorbed and repressed—in other words, no longer consciously perceived in the course of time. We nonetheless continue to register the vibrations surrounding us through the emotional body. The result is that we bend over at the stomach to a greater or lesser extent, and we attempt to protect the solar plexus by covering it with our arms. The gesture that is supposed to afford us protection, however, has the opposite effect. The solar plexus center atrophies as we no longer permit it to work in its natural way, that is, by emitting energy of its own.

As soon as we let ourselves become illuminated by the eternal white light of our Higher Self, all anxiety dissolves. We cannot heal our emotions by accusing our partner of being wrong and asserting that we are right. We can only be healed if we work on ourselves, if we focus our emotional and spiritual orientation on the Higher Self, on the divine inner energy. This includes making our own choices as to how our energy becomes involved with the universal energy and vice versa.

In truth, we have no worldly possessions, whether we are rich or poor, big or small, black or white, sick or healthy. We only possess the capacity to be integral, whole beings, to live as conscious beings making voluntary and intentional decisions according to the guidance of our inner light. Thereby we access ecstatic and multidimensional states of consciousness that render us independent of the world's reactions. Our potential is a spiritual potential. It is up to us whether or not we make a wonderful work of art, a harmonious and beautiful thing out of our lives.

✔ Contact with the Higher Self ✔

The purpose of our life, the purpose of our incarnation within the human body, is to journey back to the source. The first step, after centuries in which the yang energy dominated (the patriarchal society), is for us to open up to the multidimensionality of our being, to become involved with the formlessness of the yin energy. What does that imply in a life filled with work, family, tasks, desires, and hopes? Again, we must permit ourselves to expand our consciousness. In order to do this, we must consciously so orient our lives on all levels—emotions, thought, action. We must—and can—regain our confidence that we are part of the divine power, that we feel within ourselves the flow of divine forces and knowledge. This work is at the center of what we do at the Light Institute. In the Nizhoni School for Global Consciousness, we are particularly concerned with the divine flow in the fields of education and training for young people. Contact with the Higher Self is always the first step.

Using the expression the *Higher Self* gives us a tool with which to work at experiencing an active relationship with the illusive, unmanifest soul. In truth, our soul is not only inaccessible to our physical realm, but it is an individuated, pure energy of universal divine source; a truth of which our intellects cannot conceive. It is the One of creation. The Higher Self serves as the megaphone of the soul that accompanies us into body and allows us to commune with divine guidance from our human perspective, if we have the energetic awareness to do so. We must give ourselves the permission. We must say, "Yes, I want to make contact. I will risk opening myself to the Higher Self. I will surrender to the divine power within me." Part and parcel of this is, of course, the courage to admit even on an experimental basis that there is such a thing as divine power and that it might be of some influence within us. Truly, everything is a question of one's own consciousness, one's own way of thinking. Many thousands of people around the world, perhaps even hundreds of thousands, have experienced that they are permeated by light, that they receive answers from within, as an echo to their search and their questions regarding the Higher Self.

In this attempt to align ourselves with cosmic powers, our Higher Self can aid us. With its help, we can bridge the gap into the unmanifest. Gradually forms will emerge from the formlessness, forms that our consciousness can absorb in order to grasp and realize its holographic essence. It is a bit like a closed circle. Even the limited ego can be used as an instrument to overcome itself and to open up to the unlimited divine energy. Birth and death occur again and again in identical or similar cycles, as the soul's expression incessantly redefines and refines itself through life.

Opening to the spiritual self can manifest rage at being in body. When I first tried meditation as a spiritual exercise, I tried to make sure that my four children were busy with something or other so that I would be able to close the door behind me and return to the feeling of bliss I had as a child. Sometimes, when I was deep in meditation, the children somehow perceived the flow of energy that filled me. Then they would be drawn to me like the children in the story of the Pied Piper of Hamelin. Despite the fact that I had told them to never, ever disturb me during meditation, they kept coming in anyway. I noticed that I often reacted very violently and screamed at them. The more I was absorbed in that feeling of profound loving, light-filled energy, the more violent were my reactions to being disturbed. I also noticed that I was often moody after such periods of meditation. I did not want to take leave of that energy. I did not want to return to this three-dimensional world.

Today I look back with great laughter at those scenes of frustrated interplay between body and spirit, and I feel great compassion for myself as I tried so hard to reach something I can now experience effortlessly with just a flicker of my intent. My loving Higher Self was with me all the time!

It is a common experience to be irritated by other vibrations when one has opened up to an inner, higher form of energy. This is exactly why beings of spiritual bent retreat to a cloistered world uncluttered by daily life. Yet today the great challenge and reward will be to bring the spiritual realities into daily life and live as divine beings—in body, in harmony with all creation. If we have higher or inner or multidimensional experiences that are a positive contrast to our daily life, then our terrestrial existence can become more than just bearable.

The Light Institute's task is to liberate the emotional body's energy in such a way that, on the one hand, old patterns and emotional residue can be released and, on the other, that the creative force of the Higher Self can be experienced in a practical way in everyday life.

God and Yin Energy

As our multidimensional awareness increases, we begin to explore ourselves as particles of consciousness that do not always have a human frame of reference. We experience that *time is an illusion,* that we can become light or vibrations, that we can tap into the intelligence of a tree or a body we wore in another life. As all this comes about, we cannot help but begin to recognize that our relationship to God as a concept, a divine force, a being—transforms itself.

We "two-leggeds," as the American Indian sometimes refers to humans, have invested in God as a masculine form. This yang, male form comes with the usual negative associations of power, will, punishment, dominance. "I, your God, am an angry God," is one of the notable phrases describing this point of view. This yang energy will keep causing anger because anger or rage are forms of yang energy. As long as the yang conception of a male God power prevails, human beings will continue to consider themselves as alienated, externally determined beings. War, whether physical or psychic in nature, will continue to be considered a means of overcoming separation through control and domination until the yin energy brings the balance of merging. All of this personification was useful when people existed in passive modes, but the realities of today necessitate that every being present on the planet access divine energy and willingly use it for the good of the whole. Naturally this yang point of view represents a very limited view of the world and of the universe's creative nature. The distant, stern God has been perpetuated long enough.

The complementary energy to the yang God is another aspect of the divine power that expresses itself as yin energy. The greatest revolution of our times is the widespread search for the female God power that was hidden until now in its own formlessness.

As we expand our personal repertoire, we begin to discover God in many different ways that include higher octaves of pure energy rather than even form itself.

We know that religion means reconnection. At the heart of religion lies the attempt to annul the separation of individual consciousness from the all-encompassing, infinite consciousness. In order to reverse the original separation, we must expand our images and views concerning God, god figures, and divine powers to include essences that are the source energies of all manifestations.

Most people experience their lives as a never-ending roller coaster. Either they are haunted by the thought of being separated from the concrete male God out there, or they consider themselves dominated by an abstract conception of God whose characteristics are complete dissolution of form and emptiness, whereupon they develop anxiety that threatens to devour their very life force.

In the rich darkness of the unformed, intangible female power, we will experience intimacy and closeness, perhaps without immediately recognizing what it is. The fact that we cannot precisely identify this power, that we cannot relate it to a concrete form, produces angst. We must remember that we are born of essence and will ultimately return to its unbounded freedom.

These divine essences are not blocked from or limited to any given dimension but can flow freely across the interfaces to all realities. The quality of "essence" is the signature of the illusive yin energy. Yin energy is the unmanifest void that holds creative wisdom. This is the knowing that sources all purpose, all form. Its creative processes occur simultaneously and are interwoven.

The whisper of the future is within the feminine. It is through the feminine energy that the manifestation of form out of form-lessness occurs. The gentle feminine energy lets the elements find their way to a natural, harmonious life and growth. Yet to bring about physical manifestation, the yin must merge with the yang energy to create the surge that moves and articulates the cosmic tides.

Fear of the Other

What is true for the individual is also true for the collective. Consider the many wars that still are shaping politics in our world. So often human beings are caught up in the false identification of their egos. They suffer so badly from the separation from the common source that they go about killing each other in the name of such things as religion. Confusion and inner emptiness have grown to such a degree that most beings do not realize or know who they are in this world, how they can survive here, why they exist here. The lack of understanding of the nature of human life is so great that we seek external labels such as race, religion, political parties, social status, language, and so on. Because of our inner emptiness, we attempt to fill ourselves up with external identification that makes us appear formidable and substantial to the outside world. We posture ourselves around these labels and feel we must defend them from any imagined insult, lest we be exposed. We are then the Chosen Ones—Christians, Catholics,

Protestants, Jews, Moslems, Sunnites, Shi'ites, humanists, atheists, agnostics—and those opposing parties that we have labeled otherwise are (so the reaction goes) naturally inferior and misguided, so to be rejected and suppressed.

We work ourselves up into a state of self-righteousness and prejudice. We separate ourselves more and more from our common origin, God, the Source. Our hope for universal consciousness becomes farther and farther distant—until, perhaps, a global catastrophe will make us come to our senses again.

The ordinary way we feel and think and speak is, "Since you are different from me, you are separated from me (or I am separated from you). Since we are separated from one another, you pose a threat to me." In ideological or religious wars we have a bloody example of how we thus remain captives of our third-dimensional bodies, how we perform the most absurd continuous separation and detachment maneuvers from other living beings, how we sink to the lowest octave of feeling, thinking, and acting. Every emotional body can easily comprehend this lowest octave: "You are different from myself. You are a threat to me. I have reason to fear you. I will master my fear by mobilizing the power of anger. You are the enemy."

On a societal level, such reactions of fear are generally unmasked. Most people capable of reflection recognize them to be absurd. This, of course, does not imply that the basic fears that engender such stereotypes no longer determine our stereotypical action. They do, in the most insidious ways.

One of the most destructive ideas is that any race of people is fundamentally different from any other. This is a disturbing example of our inner dependence on outer, similar appearance in order to feel safe. The fear of that which is different is, in fact, a social lie. If humanity is to survive on this earth, we will have to readdress our socialization process to minimize maintaining control by instigating fear of the "other" at early stages of child development. We instill fear of the father, the teacher, the Church, the law, the partner, to control behavior patterns that ultimately create weakness in the fabric of humanity because people who cannot trust their own authority, their own wisdom, will become a dangerous burden on us all. The fact is that other fears, such as the fear of being abandoned by one's partner, for instance, or the fear for survival, fear of dying, and many others, are but an outer symptom of inner confusion and fear.

The abstract, unconscious rage at having been born into a limited form takes on constantly changing shapes to battle the pain of separation. It seems simpler and more obvious to try to force one's surroundings into one's own projection rather than to open oneself up to the multiplicity of life. The eruptive, explosive expression of our rage (which, in the final analysis, is powerless) is thus covering up its own original fear. Only when we feel, experience, and manifest that we are unlimited eternal consciousness can we dissolve the fear.

The practical aids for this kind of self-knowledge and self-realization are available to all of us en masse, as never before in our history. Meditation is one of them. Conscious connection and channeling through of the Higher Self is perhaps the most rewarding and revealing of all. I have included a whole chapter of exercises for consciousness; however, what ultimately will assist us most, more than methods and techniques alone, is our desire to experience the deeper purpose of our lives, the acknowledgment that humanity is but one family, not separate, but joined by our destiny to help each other through the lessons of embodiment and to awaken to our spiritual birthright.

The Hunger to Merge

We can sense what is still lacking in our own perfection. We know the physical, emotional, mental, and spiritual elements that we need to experience and realize within us so that the mosaic hologram of our life can shine in all its vastness and beauty. In the course of our lifetime, we keep taking up new elements that at first "fly around" with us and finally find their places within a

specific context of harmony to the whole. Hindsight always illu-
minates the purpose of the experiences our soul chooses to help
us to grow.

When we have achieved a balance of the impulses, abilities, and
qualities within us, we cross the threshold to merging—an arc of
expansion in which we change and evolve by combining with other
energies to which we are attracted. However, a total fusion of
ourselves with other forms of consciousness, with partners or
groups, with any other forms of life, can only be attained if we
are so filled with the power of life that we radiate it. As long as
we still lack something, as long as there is still a gap in our energy
spiral—be it that we are not yet emotionally whole, or be it that
our spirit is still wandering about outside looking for someone to
validate us—we cannot attain a true fusion. For as soon as we
would seek to merge with another being, we would either project
the energies in question onto another person through this imbalance
or suck up the other's energies within ourselves.

It is crucial in understanding the way of relationships to realize
how the balance of energy between the two persons is attained
or sustained. We have all witnessed or experienced ourselves, how
one person seems to give all the energy while the other is the
"taker." The truth is, from the standpoint of energy alignment,
that if we push ourselves on another person, that other person
will not be able to return the energy and will move away simply
because energetically we are overwhelming or smothering him or
her. Here again is the cosmic trickster: if you want a relationship
with someone, strengthen your own radiant energy, which at the
same time attracts others and gives them the feeling of enough
freedom to pursue you!

Self-knowledge, the realization that we are free spiritual beings,
is the best environment in which to nurture a productive relationship that permits at least a partial fusion. The cleansing of the
emotional body from old habits of prejudices, vengeance, and
negative emotional energy patterns is the prerequisite for attaining
this self-knowledge—not merely on an intellectual level, but with

every fiber of our being. In other words, we must live this knowledge spiritually and emotionally, as well as intellectually. We have not yet been able to experience this kind of complete fusion on this planet. But, worldwide, the realization is growing rapidly that we first must make our way back to our own individual wholeness so that we can risk surrendering ourselves to a new energy of merging.

2

*Parents as
a Reflection
of Our
Consciousness*

Our parents give us the essential focal point through which we recognize who we are and what our reason for living is. By using our higher consciousness, we can discover the true essence of our relationship with our parents and how the karmic or soul bond between us influences the patterns we take on in our lives. Spiritual knowledge of our parents allows us to experience the hologram of our own existence in a broader sense. Through this experience we will notice that our Higher Self actually wrote the blueprint for every single phase of our life, as well as for each of our myriad other lives, and that we consciously chose our parents to act as catalysts and filters for enhancing our growth.

For many of us it is initially unfathomable to contemplate that some part of ourselves would purposefully "choose" our parents. Even more shocking is that we could possibly choose them for our highest good! All too often the tender, unconditional love we offered up to them as children has long since dissolved into a resentful, resisting spot in the pit of our stomach. We swear to ourselves that we will never turn out like them, only to discover to our horror that as time goes on we think or behave like them and even begin to look more like them over the years!

This is because our parental inheritance is much, much more than just genes. Every cell in the body is impregnated with consciousness that is laden with the thought forms and imprints passed down from generation to generation. Like it or not, we are each other's mirrors—sometimes the pain of reflection simply overwhelms us.

The way to heal this dilemma is to plunge deeply through the veils of physical reality, back to conception and beyond, to find the explanation and the source of family karma.

At the Light Institute we help people to return to a point before conception where they can perceive (for themselves) that, as pure consciousness, they selected their parents and directed them on a soul level, to perform a role that would create the exact emotional and psychic environment necessary to promote the most growth in this lifetime.

With the guidance of the Higher Self, we then explore multiincarnational scenarios we have shared with our parents so that we can, perhaps for the first time, acknowledge the divine source of our relationship. Tremendous healing takes place during this process. So often the feelings of being unloved or unworthy can be shed as we review the truth of our akashic "history" together. The soul keeps tabs on every thought and experience from all dimensions. These are called the akashic records and are what the Higher Self shows us during sessions at the Light Institute. Many times, in the light of this expanded vision, we see how we misinterpret or refuse signals of love from our parents because of guilt and self-judgment left over from other lifetimes. The emotional body literally punishes itself over and over again for experiences that nurture tremendous growth, when comprehended by the light of universal consciousness!

We have actually become addicted, in our terrestrial life and our human bodies, to learning through limitations and restrictions, through constraint and the pain of separation. Thus we create unpleasant and unbearable situations that we hardly believe we will survive. Finally, the pressure of suffering launches us forward, so that after experiencing the narrowest place, we can feel a renewed expansion and fullness.

This is a very slow and tedious method of learning. We continue to choose it because our emotional body repeatedly selects its approach to feeling through the repertoire of its own experience, which is tragically cut off from the soul's knowing.

This mirroring effect of our parental relationship produces a negative side effect wherein we cannot seem to separate ourselves emotionally from our parents. This is understandable if we recognize that our energy fields intermingle from the moment of our birth and even back to conception. The egg and the sperm merged and created the zygote from which we developed, carrying with it the swirling mass of collective energy belonging to the three— mother, father, and child.

✄   *Birth as a Conscious Decision*   ➹

The unconscious memories of separation from the divine force lies at the root of our anger and initial fear of separation from our parents. At conception we move into the energy field between them, thereby separating from the higher consciousness of beauty and love and divine power in which we still comprehend, in a direct way, all correlations and realities. As our consciousness becomes earthbound, we move into this murky environment, partially or completely experiencing the maturing of the embryo. We experience the trauma of being pressed out of a warm, soft, watery, relative harmony into a world that no longer permits the same kind of symbiotic relationship as that between mother and embryo.

One of the crucial points is whether we comprehend that it is we who have made the decision as to when we are born and to what parents and as to the significant others we choose. As long as we do not enter into conception and birth with joy, we will suffer the effect of finding it difficult to comprehend that relationships can be experienced joyously. In the background, anger over the separation from our source is smoldering, since our consciousness does not remember the bliss, the ecstasy, of conscious decisions.

This is one of the focal points for our work at the Light Institute: to teach people to experience, with every fiber of their consciousness, their feelings, and with every cell of their bodies; that it is our own conscious decision that results in our living here. It is liberating, vitalizing, and enlightening to experience for the first time that our own free choices on a spiritual level have brought about our manifestation in this world as human beings with specific experiences.

Self-knowledge requires a manner of perception that is holographic and that excludes or represses nothing. But we can achieve such holographic perception only when we have raised ourselves above the limitations of time and space—when we have brought the energy and wisdom of our Higher, divine Self to bear on our daily lives. Life becomes an adventure from the moment we begin to realize our original, free choice to become manifest and to live here. Then life becomes full of strength and joy. When we no longer reject persons or situations, but begin to accept and transcend them, it is possible not only to see our life as a hologram, but also to dance this hologram.

During sessions at the Light Institute, we return to conception and reexperience this scenario so that we can perceive clearly what was happening for each participant individually—in other words, what the mother was feeling, the father, the two together. So often we have been imprinted with a sense that one or both parents didn't want us when the truth is that they simply didn't want each other—not us. It had to do with their emotional interplay. Because we were pure energy, we absorbed it as our own.

You can explore this any time you wish.

Find a safe place to relax and begin to breathe deeply into your body. Visualize that, as you breathe in, you are breathing in pure knowing, and as you breathe out, you are exhaling all the little nagging thoughts of the mind-body. Tell yourself you are looking down at the scene of your own conception and feel the perception of height. With your next few breaths, allow yourself to experience your mother's energy field. Gently enter her consciousness and ask her to share with you what she was feeling. Do the same with your father, and then feel the way their energies combined or missed during the act of making love.

I remember quite particularly the moment in which my consciousness looked down upon my parents and I noticed that my conception was imminent. I saw how my parents' fields of energy connected, and I felt as though I were stepping over the edge of a cliff and landing in a maelstrom of energies. I looked down on my parents, observed the connecting bodies and auras, and in this moment I consciously confirmed my approval, my contract to connect with them, to become their child.

When I did this exercise, I saw red and blue energies as I was looking down at my parents. These energies were not vibrating synchronistically. It felt as though they were two cog wheels that did not quite mesh—and that implied they would not spend their whole lives together. I understood that my life would be influenced by the separation of the two yin and yang energies. When I saw this scenario, a tremendous burden of sorrow and guilt lifted away from me, as I understood for the first time that I had always known this, chosen it, that it was part of what I needed to experience for *my* own growth. From that moment on, I have never felt any sadness about being a child of divorced parents!

So there are, indeed, perceptual impressions and images that permit a more profound understanding of the growth to be accomplished in a lifetime even before the child is born. And on certain levels of consciousness, the unborn child is fully aware of it.

Although my parents may not have been conscious of the fact, they did indeed invite me to come in. They opened up their energies to me, and I understood that, though their relationship had its own karmic path, we three could influence and aid each other through the lessons we individually and together came to learn.

✦   *The Shock of Sexual Memory*   ✦

It may be difficult for you to imagine your parents at the time of your conception. You may wish to reject the fact of your parents' sexual identities. Facing this, you may discover within yourself the roots of fear or anger. It takes courage to explore the hidden reaches of our primary relationships, how we react to karmic lessons, and how to recognize what we have learned so that we can heal the residue of the emotional body's negative experiences.

We need to examine the mysteries of our deepest inner emotions so that we can leave behind entanglements such as addictive behavior patterns and our own limitations. If you find yourself resisting imagining your parents' lovemaking, and if you seek the roots of this resistance, you may find you are on the track toward knowledge of an earlier lifetime, one in which you were the sexual partner of the parent whom you resist imagining loving another—even your own present parent!

According to my experience with clients, in over 90 percent of all cases, we find that our parents were our lovers or mates in former lives. Freud was not all that mistaken when he said that the Oedipus complex could be found in five-year-olds. If we deal honestly with the exposure of these realities of consciousness, we are usually led to unresolved conflicts that have to do either with power struggles related to possessive love or with teachings of the heart. This unsolved strife is embedded within the emotional body's memory reservoir and is the cause of confusing jealousy and revulsion against seeing our parents as sexually active human beings.

At this point we must consider sexuality in somewhat greater detail. Up to now our collective sexual consciousness has remained within the dark cloud of confusion. So limited to our dependence on our physical bodies, yet so disconnected to the vast reaches of manifest potential, we are only beginning to dream the possibilities available to us in physical form.

It is sexual energy that attracts two elements in such a way that, together, they create a whole new being. Embodiment takes place only by divine guidance, so we must come to acknowledge that sexual energy cannot be outside of our spiritual nature. On the contrary: sexual energy is directly connected with spirit!

The nature and effect of sexual vibrations, which are within us long before our first thought of sexual organs, are a part of the regular and normal exchange of energy waves. The act of sexuality is the external process by which the manifestation of the formless divine vibration is set into motion in this world. The sexual energy that creates the body, the first cell, is transmitted into every other cell and resonates with the energy of merging, from the time of the embryo to the moment of death. That vibration, humming in the trillions of cells of our bodies, is never diminished throughout the generations of cells, even though our entire cellular constellation is renewed by seven-year cycles. Thus, a two-year-old is as full of sexual energy as an adult, although in the child's case it is not focused in the genitals.

Tragically, we adults are committed to consider sexuality as a purely genital affair. Sexual energy is the "juice" of creation. It can be beautifully used as a creative force for any endeavor, be it art, music, building, or healing. Indeed, the healing energies flowing from the hands of healers are directly sourced in this universal creative flow that is simply channeled up onto higher octaves rather than dispersed at the genital level. So it is with priests and spiritually minded beings as well.

The patterns in our emotional body too often cause us to radiate these immanent sexual vibrations only in an inhibited way. Because of experiences in other dimensions and in other lifetimes, our subconscious sexual repertoire is still often associated with fear, guilt, manipulation, violence, anger, impotence, and stress. All of these energies are projected by the emotional body onto our lovers, friends, and children. We, ourselves, as children, absorb them like a sponge from the radiations of our own parents.

If any of you have ever happened upon your small children engaged in sexual exploration or play, you will have had the opportunity to be astounded at their intuitive or instinctual level of comprehension of the process. What is just as fascinating, given that they may have never actually witnessed sexual play in adults, is their ability to mimic even subtle gestures. The sophistication of their little bodies is incredible. Equally thought-provoking is their capacity to switch off playing both male and female parts. From my perspective, they are born remembering other bodies—male and female—through which they have expressed sexual energy.

I have noticed that the propensity for sexual abuse can be seen easily in the aura. Not only is there a succumbing posture that leaves open the space for such unhappy experiences, but there is an energy present—even in childhood—that ripens to manifest in these disconnected, sexual encounters. So many times I have looked into the faces of children to witness this "mark," only to hear from friends years later that they have had unsuccessful marriages—or worse. I know in my heart that these negative energies could be cleared from their auric fields by bringing to consciousness multiincarnational memories and erasing them— before anything tragic happens.

The many cases of child abuse are very extreme manifestations of the sexual tension between parents and children. Sometimes simple, harmless touching by the parents can release, both in the parent and in the child, some repressed traumas. As a result, we may carry for the rest of our lives a pattern within us stemming from the experience that our father touched us or our mother touched our private parts.

This pattern often is connected to the unconscious memories of old experiences. A lot would be resolved if we could accept that all our experiences with our parents are of a sexual nature, in light of our conception as the expression of sexual energy, and that energy is of divine origin. The problem is not in the energy itself, the problem lies in our interpretation of the energy as an overpowering, dangerous force that might hurt us, rather than simply a life force energy that is shared by all. If we could be comfortable with it in its diffused state, it would not become a pent-up negative force that creates harm. Our parents as well as ourselves could permit embraces, kisses, tenderness, and hugs without having a cloud of fear hovering over us. Choosing another soul as our partner is a spiritual decision, a decision of the soul. It is not primarily a physical or mental affair, but rather the spiritual effort to make contact with qualities and vibrations of another being and to potentially merge with these qualities.

The Separation of the Sexes

As we proceed into higher, expanded states of consciousness, all of us will experience sooner or later that we are androgynous—imbued with both male and female energies. On this planet Earth we have chosen to catalyze development of our consciousness by means of the polarity between male and female. Unfortunately this experiment in polarity stimulates the pain of separation. It is a means by which we explore ourselves as different, as separated, from the opposite sex.

In creating the false illusion of difference between male and female, we have had the opportunity to explore deeply the nature of each and to view the potential to master the gifts each has to offer in both the world of manifestation and the reality of essence. The emotional body pines for its lost aspect each time it is squeezed into one side of the equation. If the window of consciousness could be held open for the tenuous emotional body so it could see that it actually has both male and female parts, it would heal itself of the entrapment of desire for that which is outside the self.

This emotional insecurity is caused in part by the male having been so strongly projected outward that he must now, often without success, seek to find himself. On the other hand, the female, having previously been so strongly restrained within, now cannot remember how to externally express her feminine force.

One of the consequences of this polarity experiment is that we search for balance in external forces—our parents, our partners, our lovers—instead of seeking within ourselves. Like children, we grasp for something, the sense and function of which we barely comprehend. And so it keeps happening that lovers unwittingly devour one another, that they either squander their energies or consume them, wandering farther and farther from the integrated center of the self.

But even these processes are part of the great cosmic game into which we have entered. We use our parents to create resistance for ourselves, resistance that we then try to overcome. We impose upon ourselves a subjective reality in which—since, as a rule, the conscious decisions of the spirit have meanwhile been forgotten because of the dominating patterns of the emotional body—we find ourselves confronted by parents who leave us, who do not love us sufficiently, and so on.

This is why the parent of the opposite sex looms so much bigger than life. Their differences and mysteries are so exaggerated because we first experience them from the point of view of the child. This crossover relationship, between mothers and sons, fathers and daughters, echoes out to influence the polarity sexual relationships of our adulthood, which are orchestrated by the child's early experiences hidden inside.

How often I have heard women tell of their "harrowing" encounters at a glance of their father's penis, or men admit to still being fixated on their mother's breasts. These feelings are swept into adulthood with all their energetic impressions intact, and we keep projecting those initial reactions into present-day experiences where they don't belong! The result is fear, anxiety, and emotional entrapment.

Caught in the cloud of confusion, the emotional body "projects" all the power and knowing onto the polarity body, thus negating and limiting its own purpose for life. This is exactly why so many people are immobilized and deenergized: they think they cannot act without the presence of their opposite. Instead of using both male and female energies, which we can combine through our multiincarnational experiences, we use neither because we feel we lack the authority, which we perceive as coming from somewhere else.

The true purpose of this experiment in the polarity of sexes is to refine the male/female essences in an infinite variety of combinations so as to enhance the complexity of expressions and evolve our species. If only we could remember that we intimately "know" both sexes, our entire spectrum of relationship would be transformed.

However, the separation of an individual consciousness from the formless, divine energy triggers all the suffering of isolation, the rage against the presumed external Creator who seems to have rejected us, the fear of giving up the ego that defends our presence in the universe. In fact, we can heal the emotions only if we become conscious of our origin again and if we are willing to surrender to the divine vibration within us. Then, with the help of the yin energy—the keeper of the form—we can gain the awareness of our holographic, encompassing consciousness.

Once we have become separated from the "Sea of Bliss," we keep voluntarily pushing ourselves to the edge of new cliffs of conscious domain. Consciousness creates life, consciousness is divine energy. That is the reason our Higher Self has decided to go through with the separation of the sexes as it exists at present on this earth, first in one's parents, then in one's partnerships, and later in one's children—to grow through it and to gain awareness.

✔ *Mother Themes/Father Themes* ✔

Separation and self-discovery are to be found within the family structure. Some parents almost literally force their children through their developmental stages, so that they will become independent and the parents will become free as soon as possible. This is the case particularly in modern societies where so many parents are both working. The changing life-styles of adults are by necessity exploding the traditional models of mother, father, and child exchanges within the home.

Work at the Light Institute has shown that there are some themes that are specific to the mother and others that are specific to the father. However, we are on the threshold of a new evolutionary phase in which the classical role models of mother and father are changing. This implies that the father will enter more into the emotional support of the family, while the mother will become more of a model for creative manifestation in the outside world.

The emotional themes traditionally connected to the mother are "The world owes me something, I never got what I deserved because my mother didn't love me," and "My mother is always controlling me and won't let me be me. . . ."

The themes usually connected to the father are "My father doesn't pay attention to me, won't listen to me," and "My father has abandoned me, didn't want me."

People react to these kinds of emotional patterns in varying fashions. Some choose the role of a martyr; others delight in the bittersweet feeling of being constantly rejected and repulsed. Some prefer to be clowns, and others seek affection elsewhere. In all cases, the reaction is connected to the solar plexus, which radiates emotional energies in us and leads to the acting-out of secondary themes such as the rejection of others, self-denial, and feelings of inferiority, all entangled with feelings of inexplicable rage, self-righteousness, prejudices, and rebelliousness.

In a very general way, it could be said that mother themes have to do with fear, whereas father themes have to do with some form of inner or outer anger. We feel like victims of this anger and frequently avoid showing our father angry reactions because we are afraid of him or afraid of losing him, or because he pays no attention to us.

The mother is often more receptive emotionally and therefore becomes like a mirror as she frequently reflects her yin fear. This fear is manifest, for example, in the fear of expressing and saying what she feels. She may be afraid of contradicting the father. The mother no longer makes her own decisions, and, because of her accessibility to us, we align ourselves with these vibrations. Thus we permit ourselves to express our anger to the mother.

It is easy for us to live out our yang energy opposite the mother. It is less threatening to project our anger onto the mother and to consider her guilty of all kinds of things, since we seek out the seemingly weaker pole of yin energy in the conflict of energies and interests, in order to manifest our identity with all its unresolved conflicts.

Our self-expression vis-à-vis the father is often limited from early childhood impressions of his visible strength and assumption of power, which intimidate us. The relationship to our father takes place on far more symbolic, stylized levels than does the intrinsic web between mother and child because of the bond of the womb. Because we are often more removed from our father by constraints of expression or physical touch, there is more of a mystique about who we are to each other under the surface.

From the multiincarnational perspective, the present father may have been the mother, brother, or friend in another lifetime with its myriad ramifications of relationship.

Power Struggles

Sexual maturity triggers power struggles between parents and children as the parent realizes that the young person now appears to be a more equal opponent who does not settle for the old mother/ father roles but, instead, is seeking a new way of exploring the self through identification with the parents as an adult.

During puberty, the sexual aspect of physical energy surges up consciously and powerfully. It is initiated by the pineal gland, which controls maturation of the gonads and thus all the secondary characteristics of physical development. Adolescents radiate this energy, and parents are exposed to its unpredictable vibrant currents, which inevitably trigger reactive energies within the parents themselves. The parents erect new barriers in their minds in order to create more distance from their children. The parents criticize their children, try harder to rein them in, and control them emotionally, mentally, and physically. Instead of welcoming the newly thriving energy in the adolescent with love, joy, and sensitivity, parents are often threatened by this power and its overwhelming magnitude. The usual result from this confusing mixture of action and reaction is a power struggle. The parents act as the brake, holding on to the child, and the adolescent wastes energy that could be applied to creative endeavors, attempting to break free of the clutches of the parents. Unfortunately the rift sometimes lasts a lifetime.

We are still influenced by our parents (whom we chose ourselves) to a strong degree even when we become older. Then the question arises whether we can liberate ourselves from these influences as easily and fully as we could have when we were young— especially in cases where the parents are dead or geographically or emotionally inaccessible and we can no longer actively interact with them.

It seems, indeed, like a cosmic joke that a fifty-year-old person still feels like a small child in relation to his or her parents—along with all the side issues of potentially fearing an overwhelming authority. Since the emotional body experiences everything in an eternal now, patterns of emotional reaction that are firmly secured in it are perpetuated forever. Even the death of the person with whom we have had a relationship does not dissolve the concomitant patterns in our emotional body.

The emotional body carries within it the experiences, impulses, and values that we stored in former lives and as children in relationship to our parents in this lifetime. When the parents die, it is often merely an even more powerful reason to be a "good child" so as to prove to one's parents posthumously that one loves them—that one follows their advice, for example, even if retrospectively. This is why we (unconsciously) become more like our parents, in order to make up for guilt and especially to "retrieve them" emotionally once they are gone. We react more and more like them once we reach the age of forty or fifty, having left the rebellious phase of our teens and early twenties behind us.

It is quite an ironic situation that we first choose specific life experiences and the persons who will help them come about, on a spiritual level, and then resist the realization of these experiences on the physical level. Considered from an impersonal point of view, it seems utterly incredible that our consciousness is limited to such an extent that we no longer perceive the hologram of our life plan. That is why it is so necessary for us to liberate ourselves from the obscuring veil of the emotional body, so that we can gain a clear view again. The goal is to learn to differentiate between ourselves and those behavioral patterns and prejudices that we have taken on as defense mechanisms. They do seem to haunt us, and we assimilate them as part of ourselves.

Sometimes I am asked how it can be possible to release in one lifetime, maybe even in no more than a few days, patterns that have accumulated during many lifetimes. Spiritual seekers wonder how it is possible to become a new person in so short a time?

The answer is that the emotional body knows neither time nor space; it comprehends only its own psychic reality. In the same way that, during conception, a new being is created in an instant, our work on the emotional body can also bring about decisive changes through the timeless flash of consciousness. Complicated life problems—once they have been penetrated holographically on all levels—can indeed be transformed literally within moments. After all, the wholeness of every human being already exists. It need not be created. It is merely a matter of rediscovering it. At the moment in which we discover that we are already whole and intact and divine, unhealthy realities spontaneously drop from us.

✦ Dissolving Parent/Child Limitation ❧

Rebelling against our parents, or imitating them, does not lead us to ourselves. The shining star of our own being seems nebulous. As long as there is still a voice within whispering that our parents limit us, we shall not be able to function as masters. Since we are so receptive to impressions when we are children, we are generally marked by the ultimate authority of our parents, who seem to us to be the first and foremost power in the world. If we have forgotten God, we consider our parents as our only God. The emotional body—what we receive via the solar plexus, whether or not it is tangible in the words or actions of our parents—can see only the external parents as vital factors for our self-development. Hence, we develop resistance against this dependence and attempt, in various ways, to break through the seeming chains of parental authority. Whether we choose our later partners in direct opposition to our parents, or whether we continue to be guided subconsciously by the parental role models—if we have not clarified our relationship to our parents on a spiritual level, then parent themes will dominate our whole lives. We almost never conceive of the possibility that our parents are only playing their parts in our own movie—which runs according to the script we wrote ourselves!

It is not enough just to think about these things. We must literally clean these patterns out of our emotional body in order to become receptive on another level to our own divine, omniscient energy. This is one of the goals of the Light Institute in working with adolescents. Young people who come here usually do advanced work, and when they have recognized how and why they chose their parents in this life, they realize that they are freed from the compulsion of specific thought and behavioral patterns. When they see that their parents were partners in other dimensions, or even children, and when they see what roles their parents play in their own life plan, then not only do these young people feel liberated from the spiderweb of seemingly indissoluble connections, but their parents profit as well. If one person penetrates, on an inner level, the causes and consequences of their relationship to another, then this absolves both of them, even if they are not informed of or made conscious of the clearing.

Why? Because every flow of the soul's attention that ran in narrow, predetermined grooves so far—and thereby touched only a few aspects of the other person—can now flow out unhindered as conscious energy and comprehend holographically the complete picture of interconnectedness. At this point one leaves deceptions, projections, and compulsions behind.

As soon as the polarity in which we usually exist is dissolved on one side, it can rarely continue to exist on the other side alone. Often we suffer from the delusion that we cannot do a specific thing because some other person, such as a parent, does not agree to it. This is the cause of much anger and separation. It is one of the very fundamental misunderstandings in our lives. To the degree to which we can explore our multidimensionality, we can extinguish this and other illusions. If one partner becomes independent of such an obsessive relationship, the other partner can hardly continue to maintain it. All the young people who come here to Galisteo realize that they can no longer project onto their parents that which they must seek within themselves. They feel, frequently for the first time in their lives, a profound love for their parents that had hitherto been repressed by rage at their own helplessness. When they return home they are able to radiate this love, which then transforms the parents as well. Even if it is not discussed, if one person's heart is open, this is clearly transmitted to the others, too. Thus the parents experience deeper and also spiritual contact with their child and feel a new quality in their own love.

Patterns of the Emotional Body

The spiritual body is willing to use the emotional body as an instrument for growth and development. Once we have moved on to the level of terrestrial experiences, however, the emotional body creates the characteristic feelings, reactions, prejudices, and behavioral patterns that make us forget our true task. The spiritual body seeks the realization of cosmic law. It teaches us which factors combine to what effect in order to create new constellations of conscious expression. But often our lessons are painful because of the vast difference between this universal understanding and our experience in body. The emotional body is especially vulnerable to negative experiences that may be deemed necessary by the soul for our growth. Because our consciousness is disconnected from the Higher Self and the soul, we rarely have any understanding of the purpose of our experiences in life. Confusion, despair, and guilt are the companions of our exile from universal truth.

The emotional body is an incidental product of life as it develops; it is a deposit of the many energies imprinted by experiences and events. This deposit of the interaction of various energies takes on shape, the shape of the emotional body. It assumes a form that is separate from the other bodies. It exercises a most subtle power over us, because we seldom clearly perceive the effect of the energies stored in it.

In order to heal ourselves, we have to unroll a seemingly endless series of free associations that originate in the computerized recording system of our emotional body. We store there every little event, every emotion, every experience of our lifetime, and these contribute to the fabrication of a network that functions, in all its complexity, as a filter and determining factor for all subsequent perceptions and behavior. For example, a little boy is sitting at the dining table and every time his mother puts his plate before him, she touches him lovingly on his left shoulder as a sign of encouragement for him to eat his food. The little boy grows up, leaves the house, gets married. Every time he sits down to eat a meal, he unconsciously expects something. Of course, his wife cannot guess the reason for her husband's indecisive hesitation, his inexplicable stance of waiting, when he sits down to eat. And the man reacts with frustration and a sense of loss to the missing tenderness that he was accustomed to connecting with eating. Rather than seeking within for the cause of his feelings, he blames his external world. Either he feels that the food does not taste quite right, something is missing, or that there is something wrong with his wife.

This is just a small example of how experiences we have had with our parents can remain with us throughout our whole lives. Unconsciously, the way in which we regard the world and live in it is partially determined by the network of all these stored patterns. It is not only the case with patterns of this lifetime, but our emotional body still carries within it reverberations from former lifetimes and other dimensions.

It is most interesting to observe the mechanisms that attract us to specific partners. The quality of our emotional interaction would change completely if we could recognize the scenarios created by the unconscious repetition of whole series of associations stemming from childhood experiences as well as "unfinished business" from other lives.

Love means being able to perceive another being in terms of actuality and not as a projection of our ego onto the world outside us. In order to heal ourselves of such dramas as "My parents don't love me enough," or "My relationships are not fulfilling," we must begin clearing the data banks of all those astral associations, symbols, and myths that constitute the network that permeates us on the level of the emotional body.

Our experience in Galisteo has been that the cause of any emotional problem can be uncovered. Healing comes by dissolving separation and finding our way back to oneness. The goal is always to dissolve our personal karma by seeking the true self. Healing can only originate on a spiritual level.

✔   *The Terrestrial Group Tour*   ➤

We are here on earth on a kind of group tour. Our most intimate partners and closest family members belong to one and the same group of souls. Our parents, siblings, children, lovers, and so on are participants in this tour group, helping each other for aeons to find the way back to the original divine source.

Let us remember that we chose our parents ourselves, knowing full well what tasks of learning we set ourselves with them and through them. According to the instructions of our life plan, no energy is ever wasted. Nor is there, concerning the blueprint of the soul's development, any incident that comes from the "outside." The careful, meaningful choice of our parents along with their genetic codes, the choice of siblings, playmates, teachers, partners in love and in marriage, and, later, the choice of one's children, colleagues, subordinates, and bosses—the choice, in other words, of all "exterior" circumstances and all the many people whom we meet and with whom we interact—fulfills a specific function in developing the hologram of our consciousness.

It will be impossible for us to liberate ourselves without illuminating our unconscious being. It is essential for us to recognize the origin of our emotional reactions, prejudices, and positionalities. Part of this is the necessity for dealing with our parents and our reactions to their dispositions and behaviors, including their sexual energies, before we will be able to attain new and higher levels of consciousness.

Of course, the cosmic joke is that those beings we call parents are simply playing the role we designed for them. It is fascinating to imagine them playing different roles in former or future lives. For example, do you really feel that your father is your father? Or does he feel more like a brother or grandfather? Does your mother mean more to you than just a mother; could she be a former lover or sister?

Our positionality with regard to our parents is one of the causes and foundations for all further decisions in our life. Today, it is very popular to refer to the "damaged child" syndrome in which the parents are held responsible for any real or psychic defects. This concept is very destructive to fulfilling our life's plan because it implies that there is no possibility to heal the damage, only justification for imperfection and the vindictiveness of blame. Such thinking and justifications land us right back in the old victim-victimizer system, a form of emotional concentration camp from which it is extremely difficult to escape. The real truth is, these are nothing but rationalizations of our own, unsolved conflicts that we project onto others.

On this earth thus far, we have chosen mainly negativity as fuel for spiritual growth. A nasty childhood and the resulting suffering and distress clearly can lead—often in a matter of years—to a powerful impulse toward independent, free development, toward a new consciousness. It is important that we understand that we often choose a tragic experience in order to open up our heart.

Again and again we see how children in an unhappy home situation do not choose to leave their parents, even though the parents may be alcoholics or physically and psychologically abusive to their children. Intuitively the child in this situation comprehends that there is some learning or purpose to come to terms with in the experience.

If you are faced with such a situation, in order to grow, I suggest you not attempt to distract attention from the issue by rationalizing. Rather, work toward recognizing your behavior and reactions on the one hand and, on the other, examine yourself deeply to find out why you have chosen this particular kind of experience, these people and their life-styles. Seek within yourself and within the other persons in the situation in order to achieve the knowledge sought. The first step is to look at the dynamics of the energy flow. Once you have begun to consciously understand some of the causes and effects of this energy flow, it will be easier for you to work at extinguishing the set patterns within yourself and thus avert the blind, unconscious continuation of the exchange of negative energies.

For our development, it is necessary that we seek access to a new understanding of the contractual agreements between our parents and ourselves in various ways. Only when we have comprehended what development goals we had in mind when we joined forces with them will we be able to comprehend the circumstances, the difficulties, and the possible solutions in the child-parent relationship. We should never forget that the purpose of our life within this physical vehicle is to give our soul challenges and opportunities to develop.

3

Realities
of the
Child

It has been my observation that, immediately after birth, children are still spiritually open. They are open to immediate, direct access of their multidimensionality. They are not separate from their divine self, nor from the mother's self. Gradually, however, the infant is drawn more and more into its three-dimensional, separate, individual bodily existence and thereby into the energy exchange with the members of its family. By nature, the infant attracts vibrations from its parents on psychic and intuitive planes. It learns how to recognize the energetic states of its parents and its environment, and how to react to them. It recognizes whether the people around it are angry or loving. The infant receives these vibrations as though they were its own.

From approximately seven months of age, the infant can distinguish between people it knows and strangers. For the first time it may begin to cry when placed in the arms of someone it doesn't know. In a matter of weeks and months, the vibrational repertoire has expanded to include a category of the familiar, as well as the quality of different energy strands emanating from all those who come within close range. Lacking the definition of language, infants respond and interact with the surrounding world totally through the perception of nonverbal, energetic cues. It is a sorrow that we have no tracking devices to register just how sophisticated their perceptual faculties are. I suspect that they deteriorate rather than improve as time goes on. We do know that the reticular activating system of the brain records impressions that teach the infant what is dangerous and, therefore, what to fear. Unfortunately, much of this information is supplied by others who react in fear in a given situation and so pass on fear indirectly to the infant.

The child is not afraid of the unknown. It would touch a snake or a spider with curiosity and interest—until the mother or the father appears and reacts to the animal. If the parent's reaction is fearful, then the child registers the concept of danger as synonymous with spider or snake. Thirty years later the now grown child still has a phobia concerning snakes or spiders but no longer knows why. Unconsciously the person has assumed many emotional patterns that were incorporated from the adult models of childhood.

At the age of two and a half or three, the child begins to see itself more consciously as a being separate from the mother. It develops a separate ego structure. This period is the one some people call the "terrible twos" because children naturally begin to explore personal power and how it relates to the power or control of others.

Quite apart from the development of new behavior patterns and thought, there is an important spiritual aspect to this developmental period. In this stage of moving away from the embracing protection of the mother, the child is particularly vulnerable because the outside world is expanding, yet no one is aware of the subtle energies she is being exposed to, what effect they have on the child, or what to do about them.

During this period, the child is incredibly sensitive to psychic impressions. If, for instance, she is in a large group of people, not only at family gatherings, but also in public places such as grocery stores, shopping malls, or sports events, she will absorb the emotional energies being discharged by all those around. Usually these vibrations are the slow, sticky energies of fear and anger. The body tries to rid itself of negative, alien vibrations by reacting physically. The child often responds to the absorption of extraneous energy by developing a stomachache. Stomachaches are always a warning of emotional penetration into the solar plexus, which is the seat of the emotional body. Conscious parents can teach their children how to push their energy out the solar plexus so that they do not receive charged energy that doesn't belong to them.

The child is also open for astral energies circling the earth. Thought forms, emotional reactions, hopes, and fears—of the living and the dead—are picked up by young children, especially during "daydreaming" and sleep. More than we know, their nightmares about war are actual perceptions of reality being carried through the psychic waves around the planet. The sensitive child is fertile soil for further patterns of emotional depression and drug abuse because subconscious experiences are just too much. If we parents understood what we were exposing our children to, we would be more selective and effective at deploying negativity.

For instance, we might realize that television is unsuitable for children, particularly very young children. The astral energy emanating from the themes presented on television sows the seed of fear in our children. Whether it is a fight between two marionettes or Donald Duck dragging a dog along by its leash makes no difference. In either case the child is drawn into a situation in which she fearfully waits to see whether the good guy or the bad guy will win.

Comics represent an especially active and, at the same time, negative mythology for children. Consider what is happening: the energy in these cartoons or little dramas that some people so blithely show their children combines with the physical rays emanating from the cathode-ray tubes of the television set and mixes with the general vibrations of the environments of the home, child-care providers or school, and of the general community. The results are a mutually reinforcing and accelerating influence against which the child is defenseless. The energy pattern enters and imprints the child. Thus the seed of fear takes on a physical form and will grow, not in the physical body alone, but in the emotional body as well.

By the age of about three, fear and anxiety are implanted decisively within a child's emotional body. The child is already reaching out from the mother's protective circle, seeking his own identity in an expanded but formidable world. This is the time when children begin to articulate their inner knowing. They attempt to share with us the magic of their own reality. Often they will casually comment upon seeing ghosts, remember previous lives, perceive negative energies, or have fearful experiences in their dreams.

Three-year-olds say things that sound very strange to the listening adult, such as "I used to be your mother," or "I remember when we lived by the sea." It is well to realize that such statements are of great importance. Listen to what a child is saying with an ear to hearing the whole story. If, for example, the child says that he used to be your mother, consider that this is an opportunity to release karma. In speaking of past lives and/or relationships, it is possible for the child to release what would become a recurring theme repeated from that life, in order to be more fully present in this one.

Perhaps we could find out what happened in the time of which the child is speaking so as to free the child from the emotional patterns set up in that life. The emotional body retains the vibrations, and the child unconsciously wants to relive these vibrations. Even if you are the mother in this life, the child may tend to treat you as though your roles were reversed and you the child of the child who was the parent. Old, buried experiences of relationship create a great deal of disharmony and confusion. If the child can never talk about his view of the relationship and previous circumstances, we may never discover the source and reason for the present confusion.

We parents often secretly wonder why we feel so differently about each of our children. We simply do not feel the same kind of love for each child, even though we think we should. This is because, on a soul level, we have a completely different history with each one and come together in very distinct ways with them individually.

✐   *Ghosts, Monsters, Little Friends*   ➤

At about age three children often speak of ghosts or people in their rooms, of scary monsters or little invisible friends. These stories are not necessarily products of the child's imagination or of some psychological disturbance. Figments of the imagination can linger in the mind only when they are associated with an inner experience or memory. They reflect actually existing energies that the child is perceiving because she is not yet able to defend herself against the astral dimension. These energies will define the child's means of expression and profundity of fear and anxiety, often for the rest of her life. When a little one says she saw someone in her room, or he says he has a playmate, do not treat the child as though this were the effect of an overactive imagination or as if there were something wrong with the child. On the contrary, permit the child to give expression to feelings, observations, and reports as a means of becoming free from these things. We must entertain the idea that there may indeed be other forms of consciousness interfacing with our reality and that, by learning discernment, we just might be able to find a useful means of exchange.

Parents could learn a great deal about their children by asking what their little invisible friends have to say. It is shocking to discover that their friends are willing to give information about people that far exceeds what could come out of the mind of a three) or four-year-old. Many times there is an interesting change of voice when the child is passing along communication from the friend. This is a kind of channeling from another dimension that alerts the parents that their child has a special gift that can be carefully nurtured into something wonderful, if the parent is conscientious.

Communication with the astral spirits of plants, for instance, would be tremendously beneficial to the entire world since we are having so much trouble feeding ourselves. The results of this kind of communication are documented at Findhorn and are a model for the world.

The phenomenon of children perceiving energies from other dimensions and octaves will occur more and more frequently as they continue to be bombarded constantly by astral energies from television, computers, and the use of lasers. Lasers break open the third-dimensional barriers between the usual physical energies and the astral energies. This allows these dimensions to leak into our dimension.

The difficulty of the astral dimension is that the monsters of a child's dreams can turn into possessive energies. It is not necessarily the monster as a being that takes possession of the child. It is the energy accompanying the monster or evoked by it that drills a hole in the protective membrane of the child's consciousness, creating a fixation that sucks him back into that experience over and over again.

When we speak of the phenomenon of "possession," we should realize that we are influenced by a more or less stereotyped image that is inaccurate. Perhaps we imagine something that crawls around us, commits unspeakable actions, and finally grabs us by the throat. In truth, however, possessive energies are always subtle vibrations that influence and limit our perception of reality in a hidden manner. We are usually not possessed by some black monster or red devil, we are ordinarily influenced by very intimate, pleasant, whispering voices inside.

Unfortunately, too many parents use some kind of control by negation or punishment to socialize and train their children. These methods teach children to see themselves as helpless and powerless and imprint the child with a negative self-image. This negativity produces precisely that state of vibration that attracts astral thoughts and feelings. The child perceives the astral energies as inner voices expounding his guilt, which can only heighten his anxiety at having been bad and the fears of being called to account or punished for his actions. This limits curiosity and circumscribes the exercise of full intellect, to say nothing of how it stops the child from developing trust in the self. Without self-trust, there will never blossom an adventurer to enrich the world and awaken the fearless self!

✔   *Silence: Creator of the Void*   ❧

Normally, parents and family react to children and their stories of ghosts, elves, or other invisible energies with disbelief, rejection, and ridicule. After a while the child stops talking about her experiences since she realizes she is not being taken seriously. The result of this forced silence is that the child remains stuck in that terrible no-man's-land of silent monsters, glittering lights, strange sounds, and other weird impressions that she no longer dares talk about. This becomes fertile ground for the vague fear that carries over into adult life. This vague fear is faceless, is not connected to definite individual memories, and yet it evokes physiologically perceptible reactions. As the child grows up she may have fewer stomachaches because she has numbed or repressed her sensitivity. The faceless, shapeless anxiety now spills over into any and all dark corners of life, ready to be projected onto any familiar or undefinable feelings or situations.

Thus we learn that safety is synonymous with control and order. Yet the happy, well-balanced child is the one who is not flustered by chaos or the necessity to adapt to new, challenging circumstances. Chaos is a constant in this world; we weaken our children by not teaching them to cope with it with a sense of courageous delight.

If we cannot, however, recognize the source of fear, we may end up reinforcing it instead. That is why the work taking place at the Light Institute is so helpful. We give people's consciousness the chance to remember those scenarios, to relive the circumstances and situations that led to the accumulation of fear. Consciously dealing with the causes can dissolve the karmic ties to them.

By the age of four or five, children often show intuitive faculties. "Average" children develop just as amazing, intuitive faculties as do particularly gifted children. For instance, four) and five-year-olds paint pictures showing an aura or a rainbow around the depicted persons. They are expressing the energies they see emanate from the persons, animals, or objects they are painting. This is such valuable information, if only we would learn to develop it. When we are conscious of these auric emanations, and know what they mean, we need not be afraid of others because we have a direct way to know what they are feeling and thinking.

One of the most touching expressions of psychic atunement in children is their uncanny capacity to recognize when someone is feeling sad or ill. Invariably they will touch the person with innocent tenderness.

Children often will casually announce that so and so will come today or seem to know who is calling on the phone just before it has been answered. Even these apparently harmless capacities seem to unnerve parents, who quickly make it clear to them that this is inappropriate behavior and must be silenced immediately.

Many of us have experienced children who have predicted the death of someone in the family. If and when the prediction proved correct, it only created more bewilderment, after which the parents admonished the child never to say such things again. By this renewed deflection of inner octaves, the child experiences an increased awareness that the world does not value or even like who they really are inside. The need to be silent in terms of these spontaneous revelations creates a tremendous amount of anxiety because, in fact, the child has not learned to premeditate and so becomes unsure and uneasy with the self—the antithesis of what we want the child to experience! Death then becomes something unspeakable, inexpressible, something taboo.

Thus, as children, we close more and more doors, neglect and repress our ability to perceive the auric and electromagnetic vibrations and to have mediumistic experiences. By the time we go to school at the ages of six or seven, we are even less willing to be laughed at by our schoolmates for talking about strange perceptions. The first few years at school are usually accompanied by the complete locking away of our consciousness from these dimensions. By this age the child refuses to admit, even to the self, that she perceives the presence of invisible beings or telepathically receives thought waves. The flood of information, knowledge, and wisdom that is the birthright of every human being, and a true treasure of light for all humanity, loses its channels, its divine windows, its points of contact by which, up to this point, it could be transmitted from the spiritual octave to the physical body and the third-dimensional consciousness. This energy now remains prisoner of the emotional body and leads to stagnation or imbalances that become palpable as a diffuse anxiety in the consciousness of the adult.

✒   *Impressions from the World Around Us*   ☙

Children are very susceptible to the astral, psychic environments around them. They are conscious of vibrational energies that they perceive in the natural world. They will "sense" an area that feels happy or sad, safe or scary, to them. They actually read these impressions from the infrared imprints that impregnate the astral fields, laden with psychic, emotional residue. This residue lasts for decades, perhaps millennia, because astral energy is not bound in time or space.

A child might love visiting Grandmother's house because he feels the familiar energies of his mother, herself as a child, radiating from the walls. He might hate his auntie's house because it has been the scene of family feuds that are just out of the range of his present hearing but audible to the heart!

Children are true sponges and will absorb energies from everywhere they go, everything they touch. It is worthy of our adult contemplation to consider the value of fighting to keep some piece of furniture after a divorce, for example, if we recognize it as something spewing old energies of our past—especially if the chair or other item(s), like a voyeur, has been privy to incidents better left behind. Ths supposedly inanimate objects become arcs of emotional association that will continue to subconsciously trigger memories for all the members of our family, including our children. Even when we inherit something from a beloved relative, we should touch the object and allow ourselves to perceive whether the energies of our loved one that are encompassed by the object are happy, loving ones by which to remember them, or if they are unhappy, frustrated, or somehow negative energies and, if the latter, if we really wish to keep this object within our space.

When traveling with children to museums, churches, castles, and other places rich with history, parents are often dismayed by how quickly the children become tired or complain of headaches or stomachaches. The answer is all too often that they are picking up old astral energies that simply drain them. It is very interesting to ask the child what he is perceiving—whether a place feels good or not to him. The answers are quite revealing. Sometimes the child will recall a lifetime in that epoch or time period and be able to release the emotional body from the grips of a past experience by simply recounting it. Multiincarnational memories often are the source of a child's fascination for certain places or times of history. A particular choice of the soul may have held a profound experience or special talent whose remembrance could encourage the further development of that talent in this life. There is no question but that conscious association with any aspect of a subject greatly influences the ability and speed of learning.

It is also true that we bring accumulated fears from other lifetimes into this one. Becuase we do not consciously remember other incarnations, we cannot recognize the source of much of our vague fears and anxieties. Yet children begin very early to exhibit irrational fears that defy our attempts to pin down the cause. They may be frightened by pictures of horses or rivers or oddly dressed people before they have ever had any direct experience of them.

In our attempt to distract them from their fears, we begin to pretend that scary things are fun. We say "boo!" and "I'm going to get you!" to little babies. We try to startle them and then laugh. Very quickly they begin to copy us and laugh, too. We make frightening faces and sounds until they learn that fear is a game.

✒   *The Craving for Fear*   ✑

Fear is the worst addiction of the emotional body. All over the
world people enjoy provoking fear through monsters, bogeymen,
and other dark forces in order to control or entertain or even as
a method of communication with their children! We observe it in
children when they are still quite small. By the time they reach
the "primitive man" stage, between seven and nine years old, they
are well versed in the nuances of death and enjoy the challenge
of scary physical activities to test their courage. They experiment
to see whether they can teach each other fear. They love being
afraid of the dark, and they stimulate their bodies in order to
experience little electric shock waves. They want to hear ghost
stories. They arrange pajama parties where they tell each other all
kinds of scary tales, each more bloodthirsty and frightening than
the last. However, when the body is suffused with fear, when the
nerves of the solar plexus receive a sudden shock, when the au-
tonomous nervous system reacts with a fight-or-flight impulse,
there is a sudden rush of adrenaline in the body, a kind of electrical
jolt that enormously influences the chemistry of the blood in the
brain. Such a shock can be addictive for the body, so that, as we
grow older, we keep construing or choosing circumstances or
situations that have this stimulative effect. It is almost an orgasmic
experience for the body. As the adrenaline shoots through our
system, the system feels alive. It awakens from a numb, sleeping
state, and the body adores this kind of experience. That is why
the emotional body is always trying to repeat these experiences
and why we continually attract negative energies.

For grown-ups, music videos, horror movies, and televised reports of violence have the same function. In everyday life we have
become so numb that we have already lost much of our natural
sensitivity and sensibility so that we find only serious shocks are
able to liberate us from our physical prisons. The constant deep-
ening of feelings of guilt, prejudices, and self-righteousness make
us long for something to help us get out of control. Under the

pressures of our daily living, rules, regulations, behavior patterns, taxes, and meeting the criteria for our jobs, we strive so intently for control that we long to be confronted with uncontrollable energies from the outside. Thus we want to experience the unspeakable, experience that which, in the normal course of events, we deny ourselves. This is one of the reasons we get drunk, take drugs, or play at dangerous sports.

It is also the reason we choose the partner who gives us the greatest emotional jolt, who will hurt us the most. We love the topic of fear. We make fun of each other's fear and seek constantly to find and use it as a weapon in our relationships. Somewhere deep within us we feel that the story of the bogeyman must contain some grain of truth, and so even adults are often afraid of entering a dark room. It is the intangible, dark thing that might be there that stops us.

If we consider the contents and presentation of entertainment themes in the mass media, we will find that we are continually filling ourselves with negative astral energies. The repetition of fear-inspiring scenarios will not help us transform our lives. We may derive pleasure from the stimulus, but the fearful imprints hold the mind captive, and this negative focus runs amuck everywhere else in our lives. It is a tragedy that such paranoia is obsessing so many of our young people today. It is not merely entertainment when we watch horror movies, music videos, or psychodramas; we actually become these diffuse, indistinct, and at the same time excited impulses of attraction and repulsion, love and hate, rage and fear. The normal, everyday processes of consciousness are opened up, not only to the impressions of the unconscious, but also to invasions by astral energies.

As long as we do not clear the addictive bonds and patterns of the emotional body, we will keep choosing the unhappy love, the tragic illness, the inexplicable fear, which permit us to live our energetic processes without experiencing our highest spiritual potential. Faced with the interminable variations of fearful images and associations, the emotional body cannot seem to pull itself out of the astral soup.

✔ The Gift of Spiritual Development ✔

The saving grace is that, in fact, we are spiritual beings and our divine source is more powerful than any astral or physical reality. Our spiritual heritage is the cornerstone of human evolution. We need to awaken to its potential and protect its conscious presence in our children.

The developmental stages of the child coincide with the unfolding of profound spiritual processes. Between the ages of seven and nine, children are in a true state of change that transforms their unliberated psychic, spiritual, and ethereal energies into physical energy. At about seven years there is a closing of the doors between the invisible realms and the third dimension. Young schoolchildren quickly become sensitized to criticism from teachers and peers and do not want to stand out or be ridiculed in any way. So when a teacher disapproves if a child mentions an invisible friend or talks about the colors around people, the child's attention is drawn to the outer world, pleasing the teacher, making friends with the other children. The subtle, loving energies of the unmanifest world recede, the door to the cosmos quietly shuts, and the child goes on to begin the karma of life.

The child develops new talents—running, jumping, participating in all kinds of competitiveness, and adopting a bragging display behavior such as prehistoric man adopted. The physical expression of pent-up forces acts as a safety valve. In our schools we offer physical and intellectual role models but few, if any, models for spiritual development. At some schools morning prayer is said, but that is not sufficient to help children realize their spiritual capacities.

Because the adult world is caught up in ownership of God, we simply cannot risk anyone representing or teaching about God in a way that does not fit our own concepts. This amounts to a taboo against spirituality and is a great tragedy in that children can therefore not be given the freedom to develop expression of their innate spirituality. Parents have allocated all things spiritual to organized religions, feeling that they themselves are unworthy or have nothing to teach their children. Nothing could be farther from the truth. Helping children integrate spiritual energy outside the confines of religion is a gift of hope for the future. Let us be clear that there is nothing wrong with religion, just that parents need not be left out of sharing this sacred energy with their children because they feel they don't know enough about God. Parents need only model for their children that we are all divine beings whose purpose is intrinsically woven into life itself. As a child learns this, she will automatically feel self-worth and thus respect others around her as being the same.

Spirituality is the birthright of humanity, the inherent, sacred gift of life. It cannot be bought, sold, faked, or destroyed. The child feels the wonderment of nature and truly recognizes the magic of creation as godly. She sees herself as a part of all that is—without the complication of linear thought, definition, limitation. Experiencing life in this way creates whole beings, fearless, selfless, happy, and capable of interacting on high levels with others.

There is only one spiritual message: each being is a part of divine, perfect creation. How we explore the infinite possibilities of this truth is the freedom and the challenge of any lifetime. If we now go back and take up this spiritual thread again, and thus find our way back to our multidimensionality, our holographic consciousness, we will be able to free ourselves from isolated and rationalized fears by experiencing a new cosmic flow.

✔ Connections Between Sexual and Spiritual Energies ✔

It is tremendously enlightening to witness the connections between spiritual and sexual energies. Spiritual energies use sexual energies in order to create matter from pure energy. During conception it is the sexual interaction, the sexual exchange, that creates the body—at the command of the soul! At puberty the increase of hormones that are controlled by the two master glands triggers the development of the sexual organs and, beyond that, the profound emotional transformation that is to take place.

We are seeded into the sexual energy of conception from whence we carry the memory of its fusion and all its vital force that echoes in each of our trillions of cells throughout life. Sexual energy vibrates just as powerfully in the cells of a five-year-old's body as it does in an adult. In the child it is a diffuse electric, dancing, kinetic energy. When this energy becomes directed and channeled, at puberty, it can either be used by the body to excite the whisper of procreation, or, if directed upward into the higher centers, it will feed the spirit and the consciousness with creative energies.

In the same way that age three is a turning point, seven is also a special threshold, and then the period just before puberty, at the age of eleven or twelve. Just as we experience birth out of the merged cells into life outside the mother, we experience the state shortly before puberty as a birth, a transformation from a child's body to a mature body. The master glands—the pituitary and the pineal glands—are activated. When we were children they served as channels for our intuition, for psychic and spiritual powers nurturing the capacity to perceive in a holographic way and to maintain contact with the Higher Consciousness. Now they serve as triggers for the energies of growth and sexuality.

The emotional body of eleven- and twelve-year-olds is wonderfully open and expansive. Their enthusiasm is contagious, as they are so loving and thrilled with the flush of this threshold to adulthood. However, by thirteen, fourteen, or fifteen years old, the sexual thrust becomes a sweeping current that carries off moderation into the torrents bent for the sea of life!

Once again the young person is in a state where he is susceptible to many-layered energetic processes in this fluctuating time of openness and vulnerability. The complex interaction between physical, emotional, intuitive, creative, and mental energies is painfully and confusingly perceived without any understanding from anyone around. The intensity of these powerful energies converging creates a window of soaring emotional currents that peer directly into the unknown universe. Witnessed by parents, this appears to be a coming apart of the child/person they have known. Parents observe this metamorphosis with abject terror as their once docile, loving child becomes energetically volatile, out of control, and erratic. The stimulation of the gonads reaps havoc on the nervous system, which is subject to new levels of voltage it simply doesn't know what to do with.

Just as we admonish the three-year-old for telling supposedly tall tales, or the seven-year-old is ridiculed by his peers for his stories of strange encounters, we also frequently misunderstand young people's sexuality and try to limit or repress their developing creative powers. This is virtually impossible. The ubiquitous confrontations, particularly during puberty, are the result of such attempts. Unfortunately this creates an impression within the young person of not being understood, either by family or school personnel, causing feelings of estrangement that too often lead to rebelliousness, drugs, and even to suicide.

Since adults rarely have any understanding that this vibrant energy is anchored in the sexual/spiritual potential of the pineal gland, they are unable to acknowledge the passage or set a course in the direction that will awaken the full power of the child's kundalini. The kundalini is the divine energy, the great shakti life force, that lifts us up to enlightenment—if we are aware of its presence. If not, this powerful flow is locked into the lower centers of the body and is wasted through sexual activity. In our society this is occurring at an ever-younger age. Thus the marvelous shakti energy, which can rejuvenate us, heal us, and transform the unconscious flow of cells from birth to death, is squandered. The chance to use it for development of new octaves of consciousness passes by.

During puberty, when the energy centers, or chakras, are developing, the vital life force of the shakti rises to the pineal and

pituitary glands, which simultaneously direct sexual maturation on
a physical level. Once in a while, the energetics of this transformation are so intense that the whole environment around the
teenager is disturbed. Poltergeist phenomena are known to occur
primarily in places where young persons going through puberty
are present. The possessive astral energy of the poltergeist combines
with the outward-directed energy of the teenager. This leads to
the occurrences of glass breaking, pictures falling from walls, light
bulbs shattering, and other manifestations of kinetic energy of
which the teenager has no conscious control.

As you may see, it is important that we help young people in
a carefully directed way so that they can use well the rising sexual
energies within themselves. Otherwise the consequences will include the drying up of these energies with respect to their healing
and intuitive powers. It is essential to affirm to young people that
they are healthy and normal, that this energy is a gift that they
can use to create new ways of expressing themselves, new channels
through which a wider stream of love and light can flow. A young
person approached in this manner has greatly enhanced chances
of leadership in the future.

4

Partnership— Soul-Mates or Partner Souls

One of the most universal dilemmas of embodiment is the awareness of aloneness. Procreation as a combined effort seems to have made an indelible mark on us all, such that we hungrily seek (as do the sperm and the egg) that spark of fusion that creates the whole. The moment the child enters the socialization process and becomes aware of the "others," she begins to focus outside the self and to seek companionship, although from the very first the effort is wrought with the struggle to please, to conform, to own, to be chosen. The more we engage in relationship, the more the emotional body awakens the sensory awareness of feeling—feelings of joy, anger, ecstasy, bewilderment. We identify these with the interplay between ourselves and others and become so accustomed to the way they fill up our daily experience that we are utterly lost without them—even if they bring us sorrow or unhappiness.

Thus the dance of relationship begins early in life and consumes much of our energy until the end. We resist with all our might to be alone, always seeking the elusive "soul-mate" who will understand who we truly are and keep us company so we will never have to be lonely. Our emotional insistence that such a mythical creature exists is so deeply ingrained that one wonders if the great cosmos is playing a joke on us and this special energy we seek is nothing more than Mother Nature craftily insuring that the sperm will, indeed, lust for the egg and thus orchestrate the future. Perhaps this cosmically induced lust is the basis of all relationship in the body, echoing outward until we dream we have linked up with the soul!

But, alas, our soul is, in effect, driving us onward through the gates of earthly experience to enrich its own repertoire. Its plan to hook us up with any other souls must always be suspect to motives of its own that will always include "teachings." These other souls, then, become the vehicle through which we are taught. All too often our blessed soul is bent on teaching us such things as compassion, surrender, and detachment, by means of emotional experiences so difficult or heart-wrenching that we have great difficulty claiming any participation or knowledge of it ourselves. Who takes the brunt? Who turns the screw? Who does the deed? Our soul-mate! Our accomplice in growth. Not the one who takes us to dizzying heights of ecstasy, but the one who makes us swallow the bitter medicine—all for our highest good!

Only a soul that is full of love for us will be willing to teach us a painful lesson, a lesson that we choose ourselves. We often wander through many lives in groups of souls with whom we have a powerful connection through spiritual love. When we meet again on earth, we are powerfully attracted to each other, and we want to gain or claim each other in the outlandish, dramatic style of the emotional body. Since our strongest, surest sense of ourselves is in the lower chakras where we hold our sexual energy, we project those feelings onto the other, very often with tragic results. This physical identification is too limiting for souls whose communication has already woven together the threads of lovers and friends, parents and children.

People tend to believe they have to have a sexual relationship in order to feel deeply. Yet souls are coming together all over the planet, and little of that union has to do with the genitals. Until we are aware of what is happening on a soul level, we will continue to experience many very painful lessons about letting go. Those special connections are not necessarily here to be our partners in body, but to awaken our recognition of our soul families who are here to carry out corresponding missions of an evolutionary nature. The lesson to be learned is how to recognize each other on the soul level, how to let our hearts meet.

In any case, sexual relationship without communion of the heart contains highly destructive forces. We may hope that the long-sought-for, ideal partner is the one with whom we can live in total harmony and oneness on this planet. In truth, our true soul-mate is much more probably that person with whom we experience the most intensive karmic exchange. If we stop and consider the concentrated spiritual energy that becomes manifest in the process of conception, in the merging of two cells that create a new life, we can imagine how strong the attraction can be between two souls that have traveled together throughout aeons. Our terrestrial consciousness acts as a captor, permitting only very linear and limited models of perception because it doesn't remember our Source. We feel our mental nature, we feel our sexual nature, but our repertoire of ways to focus on and express the whole reality, the hologram of life, remains tremendously filtered in the third dimension. That is why we must let the energies rise up within ourselves, from the lower chakras to the higher ones, so that we can attain a meeting of the hearts. When we have learned to comprehend our partners on a spiritual level and to enter into the dance of the souls, then we will be capable of freeing ourselves from the oppressive despair that we owe them something or they owe us, that we are indissolubly bound to one another in an obsessive relationship.

To let go of another person does not mean to lose that person. We can never truly lose anyone. Having developed our own entity does not dissolve our commonality of source with other souls. The concept of separation is an erroneous conclusion left over from the experience of taking on form. Yet at the instant of conception, where the formless becomes manifest, we could embrace the power of the merging sperm and egg, rather than grieving for our universal essence. What a powerful metaphor for life; let go and become— embrace what is! The pulse of the cosmos seems to be from fusion to release, from birth to death, from energy to matter and back again. Nothing is lost, everything is in constant flux, transformation, evolution.

The cosmic joke is that our souls are all enjoined. If we practice opening our hearts, we will be able to achieve a new oneness on a spiritual plane, not only with one other person, but with more and more inhabitants of this planet earth. Gradually, then, we will become open to a global consciousness. How deeply we can merge with other souls depends to a great extent on the realization of our own wholeness. Whenever we need something, some feeling from another person, when we try to pull something from the other person into ourselves, we lose our balance. Such an imbalance will create tensions in our relationships. The tension that stems from our needing another person in order to survive our own sense of aloneness is an expression of the inner separation from divine energy. Only when we no longer, consciously or unconsciously, demand or want something from the other person can we experience a true merging—only then can we embrace our soul-mates.

✎   ***Healing Pain Inside***   *✎*

The choosing and not choosing of each other is very painful. It feeds on the desperation of loneliness that begins in childhood when we lose the comfort of communication with the Higher Self. Set adrift on the sea of interpersonal relationships, we are constantly drawn back into the reflection of that separation through the mirror of the emotional body that looks into the eyes of others and sees the fear of alienation, which it immediately identifies as its own.

If we cause pain to someone else, we have to heal this pain in ourselves. If our love were all-inclusive of soul energies, we would not have to reject or be dealt rejection because soul recognition allows us to connect with each other in unlimited ways. Unfortunately the basis for our emotional relationships is frequently stuck in astral, karmic levels.

All too often our energy toward others expresses itself vibrationally on addictive levels of control and dependency. Bonds and addictive relationships always have to do with possession, with the claim, "I want to possess you. I want to have you." This holds true especially of our sexual relationships. Sexual energy easily entraps because it can literally pierce the aura and flood the other person. Then the individual integrity of each aura cannot be maintained. Thoughts, feelings, and energies are inevitably exchanged between the two auras and remain so for some time. After love-making our energies are inextricably interwoven for at least forty-eight hours! If we ponder the implications of that, we can begin to glean why there is often emotional as well as physical exhaustion after making love, especially with someone whom we do not embrace in the heart, beyond the sexual octave. This is why illicit affairs are so often discovered—the psychic evidence lingers in the energy field for so long and is easily detected by its astral, emotional charge of guilt and anxiety.

Thus, if we are in a relationship that has produced hurt feelings and pain, we must clear our auric fields of this extraneous energy. If we can recognize the purpose of our conflicts or hunger for others on a soul level, we can avoid projecting our own karmic lessons onto them and inflicting wounds we will ultimately have to heal ourselves. By searching for the "gift" offered to us from each person in our life, we can develop a new, broader under-standing of yin and yang, of male and female, of the spiritual, emotional, and physical realities that lend richness and growth to our magnificent souls.

Emotional Reactions

The search for soul-mates goes on in unceasing surges, despite the fact that we may be already entrenched in long-standing involve-ments. It is a cosmic dance of alignment that we do with each person we meet, no matter their sex or age or our relationship status.

Our unquenchable emotional body tirelessly attempts to identify a point of reference from which to engage the other person. It will, of course, explore sexual avenues first, as it can so easily experience itself through the osmosis of combining auric fields. Perhaps we meet someone who will in the future become a lover. We sense an uncanny, immediate emotional reaction. This most probably results from a recollection of the past. We all have had the experience of déjà-vu upon meeting someone purportedly for the first time and being flooded with a warm, happy feeling as if we had known that person forever.

When we first meet another person, there is a subconscious search through our psychic memory banks to identify the energy radiating from them that will signal the category of response we may have toward them, such as friend or lover. Perhaps the specific framework of memory has been built up gradually through many lifetimes of encountering that being. Our incredible perceptive capacities monitor all the gestures and bearing of the person, the inflection of their voice, and so on, scanning for cues about who they are to us and how we should approach them. The brain searches its data banks extensively and instantaneously to render a verdict as to the best response, among a number of responses that matches its impression of possibilities from the cues given by the person.

The correlation of these cues may be triggered by references to prior experiences with different people, perhaps comparing traits to a stereotyped ideal or icon of a person. This is where the emotional body gets us in trouble because of its propensity to free-associate. For example, perhaps your father always made a slight inclination of his head to the left when he was about to say or do something tender toward you. As an adult you meet a man who smiles at you and tilts his head in the same manner. Subconsciously anticipating a gesture of intimate tenderness, you reach out and incline toward him, whereupon he stiffens and draws back. You feel an immediate sense of rejection and anger, though ostensibly you are in the middle of a business discussion. You begin disagreeing with him where a moment ago you thought his ideas were good. As regards partners, we reach silent but instantaneous agreement concerning the interaction, the way in which the yin and yang energies will be used, at the moment of that first meeting, at the first look into each other's eyes.

Though people maintain, "Had I known this or that about my partner, I would never have married him [or her]," this is simply not so. With lovers, the first moment of acquaintance supplies the subtle knowledge of what kind of relationship we will have together. In fact, we picked them precisely so that we could engage emotionally in exactly the ways they trigger us. We can't seem to prevent ourselves from being seduced into some behavior patterns that the partner unwittingly elicits in us. It is an age-old game to maneuver someone into playing a role that allows us to react as if it were they forcing us to respond in only this one way, when unconsciously that is our intention in the first place. For example, many women commonly manipulate men into leaving them so that they are justified in blaming the man, when all along the woman secretly wished she were free.

The magnetic force that draws us back into the repertoire of reactions to someone's energy comes from a much deeper place than just this one lifetime. The emotional body's affinity for repetition forces us into the purgatory of the vicious circle, wherein the future is molded from the ingredients of the past. The healing of emotion depends on our capacity to dissolve and release the past, bestowing upon us the freedom to be absolutely new and unique each moment of every day.

Partners and Karma

The most commonly observed problem in relationships today stems from the fact that partners are used as mirrors onto which we project our fears and emotional themes. In the same way that we choose our parents to be the tricksters of our growth, we also choose our partners to help us work through our karmic lessons. Through our habit of learning from negativity, we attract precisely those vibrations that amplify the patterns we most need to clear. Thus we see in our partners those attributes we most dislike and deny in ourselves. If we are in a destructive relationship with another person, we must realize, deep within ourselves, that the victim-victimizer relationship is founded upon a mutual contract.

In truth, the tactics of projection are some of the most resistant blocks to enlightenment because of the inability to distinguish ourselves from the other person. If we could recognize how we entrap our partner to play various scenes so we can dramatize the caricature of our emotional body, we would begin to see how humorous we "two-leggeds" really are.

What a great cosmic friend our partner is to suffer mediocrity and smallness on our behalf! I always suggest, as an exercise of recognition, placing the picture of the honorable opponent up where you can see it and, with each viewing, expressing the chant, "I thank you," as you give a little bow. At first you may express anger or sarcasm, but ultimately you will feel the truth and no-bleness in the gesture accompanied by a deep stirring in the heart. What is even more surprising is the sense of power that comes from taking initiative in relationships.

The age-old projection process of understanding is too slow for the needs of today's world. A universal quickening of consciousness is urgently needed in order to carry out the ambitious projects our souls have set out for us on a global level. We cannot hope to contribute to the planet while we are entrenched in personal karma. Not only does the mirroring effect distract us from clarity, it simply doesn't facilitate full functioning of each individual soul present on earth. We must carry our individuation to its limit so that by knowing the self we can merge together emotionally, politically, and spiritually on a global level. The necessity of this initiation of the self has become the lonely cry echoed around the world. Yet the purpose of this aloneness is to recognize that we are never separated from our divine Higher Self, and by being nourished in this way, we can come together with others in entirely new ways. This is only the dawn of relationship!

As long as one's consciousness is undeveloped, as long as one is not filled with love and empathy, one cannot escape the karmic treadmill. But at the moment in which one's consciousness expands sufficiently to take up connection with the cause of karma, which is the source of guilt, at the moment in which we consciously comprehend our inner imbalance and release it from its source, we can instantly dissolve karma.

As soon as we recognize that it was our own decision to misuse power or to act in opposition to divine laws, as soon as we have grasped the themes of our karma, we regain the power of choice to change it. It is not possible that there exists in this universe a poison to which there is no antidote.

The widespread experience of divorce is coming about because of a mass liberation from karma: we have become capable of letting the relationship of karma run out. Freedom has become a major theme explored by individuals, cultures, and societies. In the future we will move together without the friction of resistance, by merging, not by struggling, with the awkward stance of tandem force.

The celestial energies that have begun new cycles of influence on the planet have ignited the fires of growth for us all. Unfortunately they spark different individuals at different moments. This makes it especially difficult for couples to share the upheavals that growth brings with understanding and compassion. As one partner dissolves negative emotional patterns, the other often becomes anxious and resistant because the change in one creates a void of the habitual emotional exchanges between the two of them that feels like losing someone. In fact, it allows us to come to closure with the parts of us that don't bring merging and to begin again on a higher level more conducive to enlightened exchanges.

Often the feeling on the part of one partner is, "I want to develop. I want to be freer. I want to explore my spiritual self. I want to find out who I am." Quite frequently the other partner shows resistance to this. He or she simply does not want anything in the relationship to change, especially the way in which the two relate to each other.

Almost all contracts we enter into with those close to us have to do with such things as bondage, control, and paying old debts. In some relationships the primary force of attraction is not love or sexuality, but pure vengeance left over from other times or projected from other relationships.

Unconsciously both partners feel that the other has enough feelings of guilt by which he or she can be manipulated. Almost regardless of how deeply and comprehensively an old debt has already been repaid, the thirst for revenge does not lessen. In order to heal this, we must seek the source of our connection. To achieve the transmutation we crave, we try to turn our power over to an outside authority. There are no masters of karma or fate that could be more powerful than our own Higher Self, our own inner, spiritual knowing. Ultimately we are the only ones who can forgive ourselves, the only ones who can dissolve our own karma. In the last analysis we cannot become masters as long as we have not taken up the staff of responsibility. We need to become, not an object of this force, but a conscious participant. After all, the emerging divine power in us has the creative energy not only to create the new, but also to dissolve the old. The responsibility for ourselves also includes cognition of truth, with all its ramifications. We will be free at that moment in which we are willing to forgive ourselves and others and to penetrate the patterns of our emotional body with the divine light of our Higher Self.

The Problems of Separation

Detaching ourselves from the intertwining of our emotional body with the emotional bodies of family members and/or partners, dissolving old karmic relationships with them, and clearing our energies are all actions suited to closing the circle of our ties in such a way that no shackles remain. To clear ourselves on the level of the Higher Self also implies freeing the other persons from the karmic ties. For instance, if a partner becomes fatally ill, we may initially experience pity, empathy, and love. If a partner lingers with a terminal illness, it is possible that, instead of love, anger, bitterness, and rage will come forth. Unfortunately it happens repeatedly that the last impressions of the emotional repertoire are precisely those negative feelings. Major financial expenses— which can threaten one's very existence—can be incurred during the course of the illness and trigger our fear for survival. We may realize, consciously or subconsciously, that we no longer have any control over that person, or that the ill person is separating from us, in the process of leaving us forever. In such situations it is particularly important to be willing to transcend limited mental and emotional consciousness, to be open to the experience of entering multidimensional levels of communication, not only by the process of confronting one's emotions and experience in the present time and place, but also by working on former lives, in order to clear all themes that are still open between the sick person and ourself. Experiences at the Light Institute prove that after such a clearing by the healthy partner, the ill person often recuperates rapidly or else leaves the body in a simple manner.

There is emotional confusion inherent in every separation. For instance, fixation to persons who are dead need not be determined alone by old guilt or anger. It can also be created by the continued spiritual presence of the departed person. The interruption of daily life can, in some cases, actually increase the consciousness of the spiritual bonds. It is then that we may feel the presence of the spirit of the departed person surrounding us, and we may tend to wish to maintain and enhance this bond, this feeling of love, in this other dimension because it makes us feel less lonely.

When we attempt to preserve such a relationship, we are also tempting the spirit of the other person to tarry in the astral plane out of our need to be with them, rather than embracing their essence and all they have exchanged and given to us and letting them go. It would help us all if we could respect the decision of souls not only to define the time, place, and circumstances of their birth, but also to choose their death, which is to say, the transmigration into another reality, in the way that is most appropriate to them. They would not have left this life had they not completed everything that was structured within their life plan.

We often react to death with anger, fear, or both because of our spirit's imprint of separation from the soul. However, we do not in actuality lose anything. Energy—the energy of consciousness, soul energy—does not dissolve. On the level of the great divine hologram that we, too, can discover within ourselves, we were, are, and continue to be connected.

The best choice is to become conscious of what we learned in our exchange with the departed person, to see and appreciate the nature of the gift we were given through that relationship. Instead of concentrating attention on the astral body of that person, let us take awareness of the gift, the qualities of the person, and not only let them be internalized, but let us also endeavor to radiate them. For example, the death of parents constitutes an initiation for the child because on the soul level the child no longer needs a physical father or mother to be complete. It is a sign that one has learned enough in the parent-child relationship to be able to grasp the essence, the inner quality, of the parents and to incorporate these qualities into one's life.

Analogously, the same is true of partners or children. When persons who are close to us leave, it is always a sign that our task has become to express their symbolic qualities in and through ourselves.

Here, too, the pain caused us by this illusion of separation reflects ths stultifying limitation of dependence on the physical realm, rather than the eternal radiance of the soul. In our relationships with other people, we tend to associate their characteristics only with their physical manifestation, their body, their personality. Thus we keep the essence at a distance. It is imperative to acknowledge the essential qualities as a part of one's own repertoire, to assimilate them, and then to radiate them.

✒   *Reversal of Sexual Roles*   ❧

Of course, it is very challenging to peer past the formidable mask of the physical form to recognize a companion soul. The nebulous universal connection is virtually eclipsed by the energy exchanges of the bodies. This all becomes even more confusing when we consider that the memories of our bodies are carrying the imprints of all the bodies we have utilized throughout our soul's journey. We have not only an emotional inheritance from these bodies, but also crystallized memories of how these bodies related to the bodies carried by our partners, with whom we have been in revolving relationships throughout the aeons.

My experience has proven that a majority of the themes between parents and children, between spouses or couples, have to do with the unconscious patterns that were determined in previous lives. As if it weren't enough to revisit each other in repetitive lifetimes, we do so in bodies that change the polarity dynamics between us. For example, in one incarnation we may have shared a relationship in which I was the male and you the female. The next round you may have played the male and I the female, giving us both the opportunity to experience opposite polarities. Unfortunately it could be that in one of those bodies either of us had a more eventful experience and is still holding a positionality of the perspective of that body. Thus, although in this lifetime you are a female, you have an unconscious memory of being a male in relationship to me. So you may still find yourself trying to relate to me from the male perspective. I may find that overbearing and withdraw from you, leaving you bewildered and confused.

In this way, the interaction of yin and yang energies so often creates conflict becaue of the interplay of dominating and submissive patterns that simply do not gel with the feelings we have based on our multiincarnational repertoire.

The dance of relationship is even more exaggerated when it includes the totem-pole structure of the parent/child. A girl may realize why she constantly provokes her father in this life as a daughter because of leftover memories of when she was the father or the male partner in their relationship in a former life. During puberty the hidden yang energy may erupt particularly strongly, and father and daughter are both surprised at this new energy that may be turned against the father. The daughter challenges his authority and masculinity and, at the same time, practices her sexual attraction on him. Obviously these are confusing and frightening experiences.

The present father may have been the husband in a former life who attempted to dominate his wife by manipulative means. In this life he will tell his daughter, "You are not permitted to meet young men. You have to do this and not do that. . . ." These are fairly ingrained reaction patterns that keep repeating themselves in a vicious cycle and occasionally end tragically. Perhaps the father abuses the child sexually, or he deserts her both literally and figuratively. All these attempts on his part to control the daughter may be residues of the emotional patterns they established in the other life.

Communication with one's children when they become teenagers is often subterranean and nebulous, if there is any communication at all. In many cases this results from the fact that neither adults nor teenagers want to become conscious of the rising kundalini—in other words, the sexual energies that influence the relationship between parents and children. Both parties strive toward achieving some minimal distance and maintaining it, toward preparing a separation that actually need not take place on the spiritual plane.

We live within complex scenarios in which we wear ever-changing masks, thus not always easily recognizing each other. It is crucial that we begin to explore the profound energetics of what is male and what is female and how each of us has both these qualities within. The Fearless Self will emerge as we discover that there is actually nothing outside us, that all we view around us is a mirror of what we store inside.

The Cancellation of Karmic Contracts

How, then, can one become conscious of one's contracts, vows, and agreements with others regarding the development of one's life plan? The first major step is to accept the possibility that these contracts exist between ourselves and others. We can then begin to observe them closely in order to determine their workings. We are soul-mates to all persons with whom we are closely connected, be it our parents, our children, our siblings, or our partners in love. The moment in which we penetrate the source of the patterns and entanglements we share with them, we discover how our reactive emotional body entraps itself because it is so terrified of being in no relationship at all.

When we do multiincarnational work at the Light Institute, we ask the Higher Self to show us the quality and content of the relationships we experience in any given lifetime. As we uncover traumatic or emotionally intense relationships, we always ask if they resulted in vows or contracts. The theme of these karmic contracts always has to do with our inability to let go of each other, as with the pain of separation or the struggle for power in which we feel ourselves in the grips of a fight to survive, emotionally or physically.

When we lose someone we often make vows from the depth of feeling in our emotional body, which is in the throes of sorrow or fury, to never let them go again, to be with them forever, to avenge them in one way or another. These words may be lost to the mind, but they are indelibly imprinted in the emotional body, which attempts to carry out our intent—no matter what.

The cosmic joke of such vows is that if we seek to hold fast to them, we ourselves are also stuck fast—like the proverbial tar baby. What seemed like a delicious dream may become a nightmare of bondage that holds us back when we are truly ready to move on. In one lifetime, for example, a demonstration of love may be expressed through jealousy and ownership that might please our ego and make us feel loved. In another experience we might feel suffocated by that kind of expression, yet some guilt about what we owe our partner may prevail upon us to continue long after our passion and our ego have subsided.

Usually, what makes us determine to let go is not our compassion or unconditional love, but our desire to take up a similar relationship with someone else. Again the laws of karma are brought into play, and it may be ourselves who are in the position of feeling jealous anxiety in our new relationship. Nevertheless we must be willing to cancel the future and the past in order to be set free.

This does not happen just by mentally deciding to release the contracts, but by treating them as energy, not thoughts, and dealing with them on the energetic level. Energy moves within flows and also lays itself down like sediment that must be cleared in order to be transmuted. Vows and contracts are actually held within the physical body. The mind of the cells carries the memory, the command, that set the vow in motion. Merely a precursory knowledge of the body and its styles will give us cues about where it is holding such themes. However, you can actually do this yourself without such conscious knowledge because the body is always willing to be released from coagulated energy and will readily tell you itself.

Sit or lie down in a comfortable place safe from intrusion. First breathe deeply until you feel yourself relax. Then just ask the body if it is holding contracts and vows within its matrix. Listen quietly for the answer. You may know the answer by a change in your heartbeat, hear or feel it, or the body may go immediately to the next step and show you where it is. Clearly ask the body where it is holding the contract, and you will feel a sensation, such as heat or pressure, or again hear or see the place in the body. Allow your consciousness to move to that part of the body and connect into it. Ask the body what color it needs to dissolve the contract. Take the first color that you see or hear or feel and draw the color into that place in the body. Continue to do it until you feel that the body no longer needs the colored energy. You will feel a sense of lightness, a literal change of direction, as you release the bondage.

We could call this process the alchemy of divine energies. It is that which allows us to expand our repertoire of emotions and behavior to such an extent that we no longer react compulsively, or in bondage to others, but, rather, act freely, responsibly, and consciously for ourselves.

✒   *New Forms of Living Together*   ✒

Expanding the horizon of our relationships to recognize the scope of our deeper, spiritual connectivities lends hope to an otherwise spoiled landscape strewn with the debris of conflicts for power, embittered abandonment, and the terror of aloneness. Not a pretty picture, indeed. As we free the emotional body of the "dark side," its eclipse from the light of consciousness, we will initiate a fantastic, revolutionary era of relationship.

As each person experiences the utter joy of wholeness, we can begin to live together in new ways. When our essences of yin and yang can intermingle and blend so that we have the requisite variety of self-expression, the magic alchemy of merging will come into being.

We do not have to wait to live with a partner until we have become completely enlightened. We created the polarity of diverse bodies within this dimension to help us distinguish and enhance variety while learning how to mix energies in complementary ways. The greatest challenge of this planet is to overcome the separation between male and female, parents and children, and between all other polarities of our earthly existence.

Can we be fully aware of our own needs to grow, while living lovingly, peacefully together and helping one another to experience our respective developmental stages? As a rule we are prisoners of our resistance against lessons for growth (self-chosen) that we project onto our partner. The profound recognition that problems in a relationship have to do with us and not with our partner is a gift from the Higher Self. As it lovingly unveils the truth to us, we can see the perfection of the vignettes and dramas we have designed with the aid of our partners. It is crucial to our development, to be able to forgive one another spiritually, to accept each other, to recognize our karmic functions and responsibilities, and to love others within our souls. Some people try to avoid looking truth in the eye at all costs. They would rather insist that their partner play the scapegoat or, failing that, leave them, rather than deal with the fact that each of us is master of his or her own fate. The secret is to take 100 percent responsibility not only for everything we do, but also for whatever happens to us. Time and again one can observe how we pull and push with enormous energy at the strings that tie us to another person, even if we had long ago separated or divorced, or even if we have not been in touch for years; even if that person has already departed from this planet.

When a partner or a family member dies, there is frequently a feeling of heavy guilt, for we deeply regret having neglected to conclude the relationship in a good and harmonious way. In fact, what we tell each other on the physical level is of less importance than the spiritual communication. Naturally it is preferable to speak with another and have our communication received and tangibly acknowledged. Certainly it helps us to share our relationships in a visibly friendly manner. But what really counts is what we tell each other inside, soul to soul. This communication can never be shut off by the mere shedding of a body.

By clearing the emotional body, we allow the magnificent expanse of spiritual communication to bring us together in ways we thought were only dreams. We are in the midst of a marvelous opportunity, that of dramatically expanding our consciousness. Our task is to perform parallel and synchronic development work. On the one hand, we must get in touch with our Higher Self and expand the connection in order to remain in touch with the spiritual vibrations in everyday life. On the other hand, we must meet our partners openly and lovingly, but without emotional chains, projections, and expectations. As we dissolve the illusion of separation, we will learn to live together in more extended families capable of using the fire of human fusion to ignite the lighted path by which we can all journey home.

5

*Obsessions
and Possessions:
The Energies
of Desire*

Desire is the delicious trickster of our three-dimensional world. It is the Pied Piper that calls us forth, seeking some magical reality we don't think is within our grasp. As desire builds, we lose any sense of the self as complete and begin to project outside ourselves, longing for what is not in the present, what will make us feel more than we think we are. This is the terrible trap of "too little, too late." No sooner do we get what we wanted than we have opened up our sights and begun hungering for the next thing. Discarding the treasure of yesterday, we deny ourselves gratification and pleasure because the tyrannical emotional body is whispering, "That one, over there," or, "It has to be this way." Desire is the Band-Aid for the hurt emotional body that covers over the wound of separation, which we attempt to heal with the outside world. We become obsessed by our desires that soon take over the voice of reason and crowd out the attention of the moment.

Enlightenment lives within the breath of the moment!

Obsessiveness as an Energy Process

The emotional body forms the astral body, which is, by nature, energetic. If we take drugs or are very ill, or make love, for that matter, we receive impulses that open us to this astral dimension. Frequently, harking back to previous lives opens up access to the astral dimension in which we are confronted by our unresolved experiences and memories. All experience is stored in the emotional body, which then interprets any new situation by association with anything of similar vibration. This is a most incredible sensory capacity, to identify the world by association! Unfortunately, as the repertoire of the emotional body includes multiincarnations and other dimensions as well as untold reams of unconscious material, it is always finding some correlation that causes it to react. This reactive quality leads to obsessiveness because the emotional body views almost everything as a potential reoccurrence of something to which it has reference. It performs these clutching maneuvers in order to find itself. The emotional body returns again and again to a scene, a feeling, or even a thought, to reexperience itself, though it does not remember why. It just knows the energy of familiarity.

All the sensory perceptions that trigger recognition and familiarity cause us to stop, to focus or obsess on something through the unending labyrinth of association. These very associations lend the power of prophecy to influence our perceptions through which we create reality. This is why déjà-vu is so common, why so often we feel that we have been in a place before that we have never actually seen and why we meet people and have such strong feelings that we know them and like or dislike them.

Possibly we also realize that in some way we were concerned with alchemy in our previous lives. Then we might begin to understand why we are open to specific energies in this life that have the same vibrations as those themes and thought forms that remained unresolved in other lives.

If, for example, one were a priest in a previous life, then the self-image as priest will still be present on the emotional body's octave in the form of astral energies. If that lifetime were filled with harmony and spiritual fulfillment, those energies would carry over and influence the direction and quality of life now. However, perhaps that priest experienced profound doubts and therefore judged himself a liar, or engaged in illicit sexual activities, or was murdered by opposing forces. All these imprints would be triggered subconsciously by any association with religious paraphernalia and would cause the person confusion and anxiety about trust and self-worth. That is why it is so necessary to eradicate the patterns of the emotional body through work on our previous lives, so that we can end the compulsive repetition of the same themes.

It is easy for the emotional body to obsess on the negative energies because they are so sticky, and it likes the drama that releases the adrenaline and other biochemical responses to fear and rage that charge through the body. The emotional body loves to return to the scene of the crime, as it were, to revisit again and again its crystallized self. The extent to which a pattern of the emotional body can make our field of energy, our aura, susceptible and at times vulnerable to similar energies is of great importance in terms of our capacity to feel we can be the masters of our lives.

✔   *We Are All Possessed*   ➤

Possessive energy is the most comfortable and insinuating energy within us. It will disguise itself, try to lull our senses, let us make believe our identity is another, speak in soft tones; but in all cases it will avoid identifying itself as what it is: possessive, obsessive energy. Possessive energies can come, not only from otherworldly beings or worldly individuals, but from thought forms and emotional vibrations as well.

We are all possessed in one way or another. Everyone is subject to possessive forces brought on by the manipulating emotional body that never chooses to be alone, even if it endangers its control status by accepting a foreign energy source. Not viewing ourselves as powerful, we all too often lend our energy to another force that appears to enhance us at the cost of our own growth. Many forces control and govern our lives. Television dominates our lives, parents and partners dominate our lives. All our wishes and desires dominate and control our lives. To search out the ways in which our lives are controlled and dominated by numerous forces is not only necessary to be in order and accurate; it is also helpful generally.

For many of us the greatest possessive force in our lives is the mind body, which is itself possessed by the whispering emotional body constantly feeding it negative thoughts and fears. This astral trash is dumped into the nervous system through the solar plexus, which sucks it up from everyone around us. Thought forms hanging around in the astral dimension are as communicable as diseases, and a constant surveillance is necessary to cleanse them from the mind. If the mind is always critiquing and judging, there will be little peace or enlightenment. One of the reasons meditation is such a great tool for enlightenment is that it stills the mind.

This earth plane is an arena in which we experience everything as external to ourselves. Unlike the worlds of pure consciousness, matter seems to have definite edges; it seems to begin and end. It creates polarities of competing energies that strive to overwhelm each other. Compulsive behavior, another form of obsession, is such a pattern of competing energies. We are all familiar with the thought pattern that says, "If I don't work all day from dawn to dusk, I am not worthy and must somehow be punished." This astral thought pattern stimulates the emotional body, which in turn whispers to the mind, "I am a good and valuable person because I work hard. I work very hard, thus everything is all right in my life." But the hidden message, the energy that turns us into workaholics, is the obsessive thought pattern, "If I do not work hard, I will not survive."

So, busied in the outside world, we soon forget the subtle hum of the true self. Yet without a strong center, we are left prey to any and all possessive energies circulating around us looking for a weak spot to attach themselves. But once we have pinpointed the obsessive energies, we can transform them with our own divine energy, which we receive through our Higher Self. We alone can transform them. No matter how often someone else clears our energy field, the energy will still be attracted by us again and again until we have found our true essence and are therefore no longer available to external manipulation. The process of freeing ourselves from possessive energies and obsessions is similar to that of clearing and harmonizing the emotional body: we resolve our own behavioral patterns, our craving for these energies, by allowing the flow of the divine light. That which we have in common with the possessive energies will disappear if we get in touch with higher vibrations, if we embrace our Higher Self in an ever more conscious manner and trust in its guidance. It is our focusing on these possessive energies that gives them life through a symbiotic combination of forces.

Possessive energy is like a parasite. Without our collusion, it cannot survive. It will have to change if we change.

Perceiving these outside energetic influences on and in us, permitting light flows of consciousness, not only liberates us from obsession, but also arrests the loss of energy from which we suffer because of our leaking auras. Happily, within a short time we feel fresher, stronger, newer. With our consciousness we can create the ascending energy spiral that lets us ascend, leave behind the influence of obsessive energies, and become masters of our own lives by making *conscious* decisions.

✔ Ending Relationships ✔

The energies of our obsessive relationships with important people in our lives is carried or held in physical, material objects as well as within the emotional body itself. Everything a person touches or wears becomes imbued with that person's energy vibrations. Thus we can receive the energy of others through a ring, a picture, or a letter. Each possession of another's that we have is a crystallization of his or her energies. The transmission of these very delicate energies is accompanied by an astral "occupancy." So we must decide whether we want to take up these energies and whether their influence will be useful for our development or not.

If we get divorced, for instance, and we keep the bed we slept on together, every night as we sleep the astral energy of our former partner moves in and out of our auric field. This can be an important factor in our lack of peace and inability to clear the person and go on with our life, even though we are completely unaware of it. We lie in bed and go over and over conversations and emotions we have had, simply because our subconscious is being stimulated by the energetically impregnated bed that becomes an inescapable bridge to the past.

Through our consciousness we can clear the energy of the bed or the objects by meditating on them and releasing all the imprints. Sprinkling saltwater over the bed will also discharge old vibrations. There is some skill involved in this, however, and we must realize that our emotional body does not truly want to release its attachment to these old energies if we have not done some kind of work to dissolve the relationship on a spiritual level. Often the best choice is not to cling to the shared objects, to start again completely fresh and surround ourselves with things that represent only our own style and therefore invite new people and experiences into our lives. If we remain stuck within old surroundings and energy, we simply will not attract new people because unconsciously they can feel that the space is taken up with some other presence.

We must dispose of those objects in a very careful manner, because the way in which we separate from them can influence the karma between ourself and the other person. So much depends on our state of mind and our purpose in freeing ourselves of the objects that carry the emotional, astral energy of others.

One choice is simply to return the objects in question to the other person. Or, we can ask the other person to give back our own possessions. This way we detach ourselves from unconscious psychic, emotional influences and from unresolved problems and complicated chains of energy.

Ideally the intention is to completely release our karmic partners with acknowledgment of the gifts they have given us in terms of spiritual, emotional growth—and to do this not with vengeance or denial, but with a powerful burst of freedom. It is very important to be utterly clear about whether one wants to separate from a person and, if so, to do it completely. Our intention must always read loud and clear. For example: "I have concluded this relationship completely for this lifetime. We no longer have anything we need give each other on a spiritual octave, so I break away from you completely, and liberate you from whatever roles you were playing for me. Whatever function you took upon yourself with regard to me—for example, being financially responsible for me or taking care of our children—whatever connections formerly existed between us, my spirit releases you and me to follow our own paths in this lifetime, independently of each other."

We always can and must ask of our Higher Self, "What is the essence of the 'contractual connection' with this other person according to our respective life plans?" "What are the functions that this person fulfills for me?" Thus we achieve clarity about our life goals, and we develop the necessary power of differentiation that recognizes the influence of another person or people.

"Bioconnections" can be very useful if we know how to use them. For instance, when we wish to expand our global consciousness or to heal, we can make contact with individuals or groups through the facilitation of a bridge of consciousness in the shape of physical photographs or other objects. We then use these bioconnections in order to focus on their physical or emotional state. This should only be done through the higher chakras, though, through access to our inner knowledge, not on the octave of the emotional centers that we are trying to liberate from these mutual emotional burdens. One can heal the emotions of others only as one has healed one's own. It is a divine energy, a spiritual consciousness common to us all, that connects human beings and all of creation. This common factor, this exquisite spirituality, need not be altered or dominated; it is eternal.

⚮ *Collective Obsessions* ⚮

Individual obsession leads to collective obsession because our individual feelings so readily influence each other through the psychic channels of our energy fields. These energies stimulate primeval survival mechanisms that lead to global fear. Whether it is a being or a thought form that controls the world, from Hitler or Stalin to some of our contemporaries, we can name sufficient examples that represent this phenomenon. Their message is, "Our race is superior to any other race," "This culture is more valuable than that one," and so on.

Obsessive thought patterns and energies are as old as humanity itself. If we can rid ourselves of them on an individual basis, we can also rid ourselves of collective obsessions in families, societal groups, and even on the whole planet. The basic pattern of social and political fear is still much too frequently "If you are powerful, I cannot be powerful—only one of us can survive." The alternative, to which we have not been open enough to date, means turning toward each other, dealing with each other like a harmonious family, thereby giving up individual claims to power and finally taking on our collective birthright.

This paranoia can be left behind if we experience our own divine selves and thereby the divinity of every other being deep inside and in a tangible way. On this planet Earth we have reached a stage of evolution in which it is important to find the inner guru, the inner teacher. We are blessed with great beings who instruct and model for us the choice of enlightenment. Tragically we become obsessed by their essence and power and then cannot see the divine reflection they offer us. We hunger to receive their spiritual wisdom, even though we actually possess our own spiritual knowledge from the time of our birth. We do not have to collect more energy or more spiritual wisdom. Everything is already within us. We merely have to make the connection between our manifest world and the unmanifest spiritual dimensions. We expand the divine consciousness by letting it flow into the physical octaves. The divine consciousness is already there. It is a question of applying it creatively. Our lack of comprehension and our abuse of energy cause the dependency whereby our spiritual energy is squeezed into rigid patterns of adherence and mimicking something outside ourselves. It is not the guru or the religion that controls us, it is our refusal to become ignited with the flame of our own divine spark.

We should consider this challenge an initiation. All true gurus spread this message, "Seek God in each other, find the master in yourselves." We want to awaken the understanding of our own spirituality. We are eternal, unlimited, and divine. As soon as we realize this, we have to transpose the thought into our everyday life and learn its practical application. We can do this only if we turn inward and let go. At the Light Institute we call this path "access to the Higher Self." Only when we have attained inner clarity and can send out the message ourselves, that every being is divine, will the message resound around the world.

If we want to move beyond the obsessive emotional level of relationship to parents, children, teachers, partners, or gurus, if we want to transpose their teachings and apply them, then we will have to detach ourselves. Through this detachment from them we reach a new octave of universal energies. We disentangle our relationship on a lower octave and float up to a higher octave in which we recognize an encompassing flow between us.

Here is a little exercise to promote this consciousness. It applies the same method that we used for clearing and liberating people from children, parents, partners, or people from other countries and continents.

Attain your meditative posture and visualize the being, person, or collective with whom you are in a position of polarity, whom you fear or are angry with. Then ask the person or collective to tell you what color it wants from you, the purpose of this exercise being that you and the other entity will release each other.

When you feel you have received an acknowledgment of the message you sent, and you have an idea of the color that is being requested, visualize a large cloud of this color forming over your head. Then visualize it flowing into you, through your head, the crown chakra, and down through your body to your solar plexus. Then visualize yourself projecting that color from your solar plexus to the entity with whom you are in communication. The color or the energy that the form asked for need not come from within yourself. Simply let it flow through you from universal octaves.

You thus experience the unlimited, divine energy flow. It is an energy that is subject to no external power; it does not come out of the struggle for survival. It can never be diminished. By entering this energy and transmitting it to that person or to the collective, you yourself become a participant in a new octave of consciousness.

One interesting and recurring observation is that when we are doing this kind of exercise, the emotional body forgets all fears and anxieties. Instead it is completely engrossed in transmitting the energy or color that flows in through the crown chakra, transmitting it in a pulsating way through the solar plexus and thereby making the emotional body part of the pulse that lets one return with ease into the divine unmanifest.

As the emotional body forgets its fears, it takes on new patterns that have to do not with the struggle for survival directed against others, but, instead, with the hologram of life. Healing the emotions is possible when the emotional body is given the chance to be suffused with higher spiritual vibrations or with the all-encompassing divine energy that is freedom. This is what all beings on earth long for, whether they know it or not.

6

*Groups
and
Emotions*

Group "Games"

One of the most fascinating attributes of human nature is our inherent sociability. We are definitely a group animal, like our friends and close relatives, the apes. Sadly we have not learned to live harmoniously together in groups as have our sea relatives, the dolphin and whales, who, it seems hopeful to add, have had several million years longer than ourselves to learn the secrets of blissful communal life.

As children we seek to move outward from the primary family unit into the neighborhood and community. Our initial group experiences set the stage for the sense of self to be imprinted or influenced by "others" outside us whom we look to for acceptance and affirmation. The teachings available to us from the group experience are some of the most profound for the evolution of the soul. Experientially, however, they are usually wrought with pain and confusion. All of us know the deeply felt hurt that comes from exclusion by the group. Whether our hunger to belong comes from some inherent genetic coding of our species that is nothing more than a survival mechanism carried over from prehistoric times, or the distant murmuring of our merged cosmic consciousness, the communal urge is ingrained early and persists long into our lives, even though many of us adamantly deny its presence, perhaps because of some painful memory—in this life or another one.

Once initiated into the group environment, we will fight to keep our place and often reinforce our sense of belonging by pitting our group against another. This is a contortion of self-righteousness that uses negative confirmation to enhance self-worth (such as, "We are not a part of that group that is different, therefore inferior, threatening, or in opposition to us").

Throughout the history of humanity, we see how different groups gathered together with a sense of common identity that they defended, often to the death, as a measure of individual purpose. Group games were created to give vent to the energy expressed by the group.

The Mayans and the Aztecs played in groups for survival. The Romans titillated their senses by watching the Christian martyrs in the Coliseum. It makes no difference whether one is fighting for a ball, tossing a fellow being to the lions, or killing fans of a rival soccer club because they speak a different language or fly a different flag. In the end the issues are the specific group dynamics that make people give up their own personal identity just so they may be part of the group. On the one hand, groups or mass assemblies give us the supposed security of a new unit that is larger than our individual personalities. On the other hand, they also automatically alter our powers of perception and our mode of behavior. The individual emotional body finds those impulses that correspond to its prejudices, predisposition, and values within the group and is capable of enhancing them to such a degree that they may block every rational thought.

Within our emotional bodies there are astral energy patterns that seem to attract us magnetically to corresponding group activities. One could also say that we possess a certain resonance to archetypes of the collective subconscious that we want to live in our personal lives, perhaps because of our multiincarnational repertoire. These patterns keep stimulating us, subconsciously, to reactivate them.

Even if the cruel and deadly games are long erased from our conscious mind, the hours and hours people are willing to spend in front of their television sets in order to watch a game of golf, a football game, or some other group event is verification of memories of personal, emotional involvement: primordial feelings whose importance we don't quite remember. The emotional body entices us again and again to sublimate its needs that know neither time nor space. Believing itself alive by experiencing the emotional excitement, the surges of adrenaline when we hope, and fear, and cheer as our heroes and team win or lose, the emotional body confirms its individual consciousness, its very existence.

We store the memories of the games we played in previous lives and dimensions within the cells of our physical bodies. In ancient cultures the point of such games was often life or death. The loser would be killed or exterminated, whether the loser was an individual or a whole group. This, of course, made a profound impression on the body, which may respond out of precisely that same repertoire today, without any conscious need to struggle to win. We find an echo of this in the Middle Ages, where jousting could end in life or death, and later on in duels. It is fascinating to note that women are as invested in these games as are men. The passion definitely does not come from the stance of the observer, but from the heat of the battle, as it were. Women have been men in other lives, just as men have experienced being women!

These group game memories need to be flushed out from our bodies so that we can reapply the communal concept in a new way that will support world peace, not the prolongation or dominance of any one group. We must imprint our consciousness with the deliciousness of variety as a delight of life, not as a threat to our survival. From the spiritual perspective, we are all one group soul. The joy or even ecstasy of a communal performance that is for the good of all and aimed against no one is incomparably greater than even the greatest pleasures of triumph when the opponent dies as a result or is destroyed or suffers in some way. This alteration of consciousness cannot be reviewed by the mental body and transferred to the emotional body; it can only be transmitted by the spiritual body.

✔   *Groups as Props for the Self*   ❧

The immanent longing and the inherent urge toward consciousness
of the holographic character of life are tapped in the context of
the group. We hope to find the fulfillment through group participation that we miss in our individual lives. We perceive ourselves
in such narrow and limited contexts that we seek the excitement
and stimulation of groups to fill up the gaps in activity and meaning.
The group offers us an external measure, a seal of approval, by
which we judge our worth, verify and identify ourselves. We
enhance and expand our self-image by attaching ourselves to a
group, which then becomes an indispensable prop for creating the
illusions we conclude are necessary to survive in the world.

Utilizing a group as a prop is very disadvantageous to self-
development because the true self is hidden behind the cloud of
false identity. Anger and fear, resulting from separations far from
one's relationships to family or partners, often find expression
through the causes, campaigns, and ideologies purported by groups.
All too often group mind justifies irrational or even destructive
acts by the measure of its own mass power alone. The exchange
of aggression and fear between political opponents, adherents of
various religions, members of sports clubs, and so on becomes
exaggerated by the intoxication of power at mass levels.

This is the dark side of human nature, when as groups we
participate in destruction in ways we would never dream of doing
alone. Examples abound, such as religiously motivated wars and
massacres throughout the centuries; persecution of the Christians
in the Roman Empire, the crusades against Moslems and heretics
in the Middle Ages, the holocaust against the Jews and the gypsies,
the murders of Protestants and Catholics in Northern Ireland, the
bloodbath against Shi'ites and Sunnites in the Gulf war . . . and
there are further examples not regarding religious creeds, but rather
in the name of a higher culture or party, such as the subjugation
of South and North America by Europeans and the near exter-
mination of the Indian people, colonization and slave trade, repres-

sion and exploitation of groups within one's own nation, such as blacks or Indians, the nuclear arms race and politics between the USSR and the United States, civil wars, revolutions, on and on. . . .

The group mask allows for justification of the unjustifiable, the unspeakable that tosses us into the karmic abyss. In all cases of mass emotional eruptions, the participants are suffering from false identifications of the emotional body with fictitious, external group formations, phantom images, and superegos, quite the same as on the personal, private level, but with a much more severe outcome.

We must return to the source, to the cause of such phenomena. The patterns that are deeply inbedded within a person's genetic structure are not only patterns regarding the physical body, personality traits, and other individual factors. There is also a store of information, of predispositions concerning the soul's criteria for decisions. The soul chooses not only parents and partners, but also birth and life places, nationality, the propensity for groups, clubs, and teams. This predetermined commitment to decisions already contains the trauma concomitant to every choice: identification with one aspect and separation from another—in other words, separation from wholeness.

The identification process and the resulting emotional energies are all the more clear and intensive as regards affiliation with a group because in a group one can already, in a certain sense and on a certain level, experience the belonging to and participation in an entity that is larger than the individual. It was the pain of separation from the cosmic whole that began this downward spiral, but the group never, ultimately, heals the scar because humanity misuses it to pretend grandiosity, thus breeding more separation.

⚘   *The Stranger*   ⚘

It becomes evident, especially after considering the circumstances described above, that a new way of thinking, an expanded perception of our consciousness and our being, can in and of itself change our terrestrial existence forever. If we recognize that there are no strangers, no enemies, no outsiders, and no "others," that all people with whom we have to interact, especially our supposed adversaries, are souls familiar to us for aeons, with whom we have arranged to meet in an intricate dance of life and death, then it would be easier to honor one another and find more pleasure in this mutual exploration.

As we develop the conscious capacity to be the witness to our interaction with the people who appear on our life screen, we begin to actually learn how to direct the play. We can move them around and modify or alter their roles to access the most poignant soul material for our growth. It is a shocking and slightly scary discovery to recognize that it is we ourselves who make the choices that design reality. Timidly, at first, we feel our way into freedom and responsibility. The moment we take responsibility—from the heart—life starts working for us. Even if we must change the players and the locations, we begin to feel an inner peace and an easier flow that comes from being on the path ordained by the Higher Self.

The Fearless Self emerges as we extend our vocabulary of participation to the world beyond our immediate family. The people who form our close karmic pool of soul friends—our parents, siblings, partners, and children—are the ones who are the most dangerous to our ego and our manipulation of truth, because they so easily penetrate our magnetic field to push the buttons that force us to respond and change. But as our world stretches out, we have the opportunity to discover the unlimited extent of familiarity from the perspective of the soul. *There are no strangers!*

Each being we encounter, even from a distance, is placed in that synchronous space to teach us to reflect on the self. It is of great service to our conscious awareness to take up the practice of observing the world by asking ourselves, "How is this reflected in me?"

We crack open the shell of compassion when we look upon the beggar, the liar, and the killer as a part of our own psyche. As we take up the power to look on the world and see it as a mirror of ourselves, we begin to find the strength to pass through fear to the other side . . . to the shore of Knowing.

This glimmer of recognition offers us the power of participation. As the heart enters the fray, we can grasp whole new dimensions of relativity that can be used for problem solving on a global level: because from the dimension of the individual we expand to the reality of the group. The earth, in all her living wisdom, is signaling to us that we must now acknowledge our mutual bond, the irrevocable link between ourselves and all other species and life forms, and begin to move together with holographic consciousness to clear levels of karmic relationships and complexities—not just of individuals, but of whole groups of individuals.

More and more people are already in the process of developing a new consciousness about our interrelatedness and are willing to take the risk of dissolving the safe distance from the stranger to reach out and work together. There are movements for nuclear disarmament, for saving nature and the environment from thoughtless, exploitative destruction. There is active empathy for those dying of hunger in areas of drought. There are rescue missions after catastrophes have occurred. We are discovering, none too soon, that we can bring group consciousness up out of the abyss of the past to form new alliances that include the coupling of great power and love, great giving and receiving.

❧   *Separation from the Group*   ➹

It is crucial for us to separate from any and all groups in which we participate to make sure that we are using them as an expression of our divine group soul and not letting our emotional body use them to express any negativity we would not allow ourselves in individual circumstances. Exploring our motives for joining a group as well as our rewards, emotional and otherwise, will help us to further know our inner selves.

It may be that we feel more powerful when we have the backing of a group. Group support makes us feel less vulnerable to criticism and more persuasive in our point of view. If one of the themes we are working on is lack of self-trust, the group fosters our sense that we can be trusted because we trust the group that, in turn, trusts us. Groups that expound strong ideals or philosophies enhance our feeling of self-worth by the acknowledgment of our belonging to them.

The emotional body tries to prove its existence again and again by grafting itself onto already implanted reaction mechanisms approved in a social format. To this end it uses identification with groups that permit the stimulation of its own energy. Major sports events, demonstrations, and even military confrontations are so popular because one can scream, cry out one's anger and fear, pretend something bigger than the self and therefore more legitimate. "Letting out" the emotions may have a short-lived safety-valve effect, but it deepens the patterns in the emotional body through repetition of vibrations that are generally of a lower nature, such as primitive feelings of triumph over an opponent or fear and resentment at one's own defeat and helplessness.

We hunger to identify ourselves with the "good guys" and self-righteously fight against the "bad guys." As much as the cathartic and releasing functions specific to sports events and other kinds of demonstrations might be considered desirable and helpful, we tend to misuse them as an acceptable front for our unresolved aggressive tendencies. The projection of good and evil as forces outside ourselves is an illusion that can only delude our ego and deny us the growth that truth can bestow.

A classic and sometimes amusing example of the emotional body's modus operandi can be found in political rallies. As a rule we already know the factual line of reasoning that the speaker represents. Very rarely indeed is there a novel concept for better politics. Still, we go to the rally in order to let the energy of the speaker give us an emotional high, as it were. The group surrounding us adds enormously to the climactic buildup of energy. If the speaker were to talk to us alone, he would not have to shout as loudly, for instance. He presumably would not generalize as much, would hold back some of his slanderous statements, and so on. Of course, we go to public events hoping something thrilling will happen: like the Peeping Tom, the emotional body prowls about looking for anything and everything that will arouse its voracious appetite so that it can feed on the life force energy of the external world.

If we are willing to explore these aspects of our emotional body, we can ultimately shed the fixation of the group. Weaning ourselves away from secondhand, passive living frees the time and space for us to develop a sacred relationship with the Higher Self and return to the flow of energy that awakens universal consciousness—so beyond the facade of groups.

External Dependencies

The inherent difficulty of belonging to a group is the passivity it instills. People tend to lose their capacity to initiate action or choice, individually. Not having to work so hard to establish an identity, they linger behind the group mask and hope others will make the crucial decisions.

The emotional body develops the habit of sucking from the world its quota of emotions, which all too often it gets from secondhand experiences, such as gossip, news stories, or television. A kind of emotional voyeurism can ensue. Like watching a football game on television, we consume indirect light and sound impressions and pretend they are real. We no longer are in the grip of immediate, direct vibrations but instead are in those of the reflection of a reflection. Twenty or thirty years ago we would have been on the playing field ourselves or at least on the edge of the field as spectators.

In a world filled with frightening scenarios, we have found safety in controlling our thrills in front of us on the tube. We engage our fears by watching them played out in horror stories and contained violence that we can experience from the comfort of the armchair. The habit of living through others is destructive to everyone around us. Parents often fill the holes of boredom and lack of real power in their lives by living through their children. With such an emotional dependence at stake, they have great difficulty letting go, even though hanging on creates tremendous emotional turmoil as the children struggle desperately to free themselves from the possessive clutches of their parents. Though the parent maintains it is all for the child's own good, the intuitive sense of the young confirms that it really has nothing to do with them.

In love relationships the exertion of power plays a different but no less important role. How often do we suspect or know that it would be better for our relationship if we did not cling to one another anymore? All too often relationships are primarily a struggle for power. Only when we dominate another person subtly or openly does our power seem to become manifest to ourselves and the world. We learn to confirm our own identity from the polarity and therefore cannot let the relationship go. We tenuously continue the battle so as not to lose the war.

In other words, even when we ourselves suffer from open or hidden power struggles within a relationship, we seek neither to break it off nor to change it. The emotional body still has to learn that it can find and determine its existence, not in polarity and confrontation, but, rather, in merging with the all-encompassing creative energies. Again and again we feel the urge to belong to something, to someone. That is also one of the reasons people who have just left one relationship enter almost blindly into a new one, which almost invariably is defined by the same themes and challenges as the old one.

We turn to the outside world to pursue a kind of happiness defined by events, since we do not experience happiness as a state of being within ourselves, as consciousness of the Higher Self. We become more or less immune to the profound energies of happiness because we do not engage directly and intimately enough in life. The only alternative is opening up to the multidimensional consciousness of our Higher Self.

✔ *Emotion, the Outward Movement* ➘

The word *emotion* expresses quite nicely what emotions are. Motion = movement, e = outward—in other words, it is a movement toward the outside. Our thoughts move from their source within us outward to become reality. Most of us have experienced that wishes (thoughts fueled by emotion) can be dangerous, precisely because they come true. How often have we experienced that we wish for something, don't receive it immediately, and then get it later, at which point we no longer really want it and may actually be bothered by it? In such cases we tend to speak of coincidence. We ignore the law of cause and effect in which everything that happens results from a prior cause or causes.

Emotional confusion is caused by the emotional body's need to live the patterns imprinted subconsciously within it, again and again. Since the patterns of fear, anger, self-righteousness, depression, sorrow, and other slow vibrations are deeply imbedded, the emotional body continually seeks situations that revive these emotions caused by forgotten experiences.

In the end, however, we must learn to sense this repetition and dissolve it by ferreting out all connections and triggers associated with it through holographic awareness. If we cannot perceive the matrix of cause and effect, we will forever be caught in its inextricable web.

The healing of emotion happens when we recognize the connection between the unmanifest and the manifest on an energetic octave. If we really want to, we can transpose an ecstatic vibration from the spiritual realm into our daily lives. The opening up of our consciousness to new perspectives is the key to being healthy, whole, ecstatic, creative, and loving.

✔ *How We Can Change* ➘

You may ask, "How can one person alter the reality surrounding oneself?" Many political and social developments seem so overpowering that the individual cannot imagine being able to alter external circumstances. Yet every single human being already has enormous powers, as is demonstrated by the fact that each soul has decided to become incarnate in a human body to contribute some special gift to the world of form. Being present on this planet in these times is indeed a sign that we have the energies necessary to confront the immense challenge of collective catastrophes, wars, and social changes, not to mention individual themes such as the resolution of parent/child and love relationships.

On the one hand, we must regain our connection with the Higher Self so that we can feel the guidance that orchestrates the flow of our lives. On the other hand, we must begin to rejoin our divine soul group and work together to problem-solve and answer the challenges we collectively set for ourselves.

We have been completely and utterly seduced by the experiment of polarity we ourselves chose to explore here on earth. We have begun to actually believe that we are separate. Separation consciousness can herald only war and destruction because it is the epitome of the illusion of survival. Without the awareness of the Higher Self, the emotional body has no way of remembering *oneness* and so is sentenced to the boredom and limitation of survival. Surrounded by this drama, the emotional body cries out for company and so becomes the seducer, the trickster, the beggar. As we look to each other for comfort, we see only the face of desire or the face of rejection. This is much too narrow a scope for the pursuit of powerful manifestation. At least it necessitates a change. Change is the bread of life. We, too, must change!

All of nature, heaven and earth, is bent on helping us realize that we are irrevocably bound together as the family of humanity and must elevate human consciousness to an octave in which our common destiny becomes a clear choice that we all embrace together. The multitudinous catastrophes that are increasing over the planet are nudging us to move together with one heart, one body, to choose to participate with the power that each of our knowing souls brings forth into body.

Now we have the opportunity to close the gap and remerge the energies that have taught us separation. We must risk moving into groups again and applying our collective powers of manifestation to our mutual benefit. As we cease the misuse of the self, we will also be able to transmute group action into loftier goals set by our souls. Change is imminent on this planet, and the catalyst for that change is *consciousness* . . . easily within our grasp because it is our very source.

7

Healing Ourselves Through Creative Balance

Balancing our inner and outer worlds in such a way that they flow into each other allows us to become totally present beings, capable of commanding reality. Tapping our inner resources helps us to experience that we are, indeed, the healing force in our own lives. Within us lie the answers as to who we are and the purpose of all our experiences. As we explore the inner reaches of our being, we come to see the outer world from an entirely different perspective. Human creative potential is unlimited; with it we can sculpt the universe.

The Child Within

One of the greatest aids in our efforts to expand our consciousness, at least in the initial phases, is to contact and experience the child within. The child consciousness that resides within us still possesses a holographic way of perceiving things and has both the joy and the ability of being able to enter into new experiences, other dimensions, and to fearlessly seek and enjoy adventures. The aspect of our consciousness that I call "the child within" is still able to move freely and uninhibitedly, not only physically, but also mentally and spiritually, without being either aware of or impeded by the barriers interposed by adult definitions of what is real and what is unreal. The child in us does not yet feel the limitations of the space-time continuum.

When we get in touch with the child within, we are able to reach beyond the usual boundaries that, as a child, we were obliged to learn to accept. One way for us to do this is by the process of imagery. When we speak of imagination, creative visions, or clear dreams, we are referring to a conscious world of images that is connected to the meaning of life and is capable of sharing the emotional body through its high energy vibration.

Perhaps this is an odd simile, but consider the tadpole, whose dream is to be a frog. Outwardly the two images are almost completely different, as are their dwelling places, activities, and diet. Yet through the magic of Kirlian photography or the reading of its aura, the dream of the tadpole becomes actually visible and provable to the eye that is aware and enhanced. It really exists! We may think of other dreams as well, the dream of the egg, the chrysalis, the seed, the bud. Each dream is a step, lifting the being beyond, and while the being itself sleeps within the dream, it acts in a waking state, unconscious of the dream and its destiny yet following the immutable laws laid down by the dream that it chose prior to incarnation, so that the tadpole, marvelously entwined with the miraculous, becomes again the dream of the frog, through the mechanism of the egg.

When you were a child, were you in touch with other senses, other levels of awareness, colors, feelings, a sense of the presence of another or others? Did you have dreams—dreams you were not able to share, perhaps, with anyone? Over the years these dreams may have been thwarted, frustrated, mocked, forgotten, or overlain by many accretions of experiences, intentions, choices, and obedience to various dictates of parents, school, society, and so on. They are still there, deep within you. As a child you know you had pleasures and joys, interests and delights. To see a little child in the parking lot of a shopping mall, enchanted by the sparrows hopping under cars, which the adults pass by without a glance, or to glimpse wonder in the eyes of a baby who stares at the light in the refrigerator door, is a reminder of a precious energy that is still a part of us now. The child within is never lost, it is just separated by our adult mind, which throws away today as it obssesses on yesterday and worries about tomorrow.

The child within will show us what it loves to do and the experiences toward which it most wishes to gravitate. For instance, I experience now just how much the child within me likes to touch people's consciousness—how she loves to be in the presence of so many Higher Selves, fly into the sky, communicate with energies of rocks, animals, and other dimensions. Also, in terms of future prescience, when I was a little girl wondering about what my future life as an adult would be like, I could see myself in an adobe house. At the time I did not know what adobe was, but I had a clear picture of myself in that funny little brown house. People went in and out, I laughed, touched them, and felt how they were changing. Since I did not repress these experiences as a child, the energetic processes that have realized their vibrations were able to develop within me.

Each of us has special gifts to call upon that enrich our lives and assist us in the quest of our souls. Have you any such memories or recall of pictures you had as a child that have now become reality in your present life? Can you experience pleasure now from something that delighted you when you were little—not just as a memory, but as an actuality?

The child within has access to the source of knowing that brought us into being across the threshold from the unmanifest into this world. In sessions at the Light Institute we facilitate the inner child to point out to us these talents and knowings that bring about a profound balancing, simply because we remember the power of creating action ourselves. The heart-lifting dialogue with the child about our choice to enter into this life and discover the gifts of growth always makes us feel strong and peaceful to be who we are.

Pictures, Perception, and Reality

We play with our consciousness in many ways. There is the delicious pleasure of daydreaming as we lie on our backs, gazing at clouds endlessly moving, melding, changing shapes against a bright blue sky, or perhaps staring deeply into thundering and receding ocean waves, or the spray and fluidity of a waterfall. Even while paddling and bobbing about in the ocean or a lake, there comes a strange sense of connection with all the amoeba, plant life, and fishes in that body of water. Maybe, while galloping among a group of horsemen, the sound of hooves and the speed and motion of the horse, coupled with strong feelings, brings an awareness of a connection with horses and horsemen through many aeons.

In our evolution as humankind, certain nebulous memories of multidimensional conscious lives become almost everyday experiences. Barrages of other lives are all around us, bursting against our consciousness like waves against the shore. Many people have turned to drugs, hoping to touch ecstasy, to expand their awareness. Members of certain religions, such as the Sufi dervishes, adopt other methods to break the third-dimensional barriers imposed by the rigorous demands of various forms of civilization. Among members of Western society, more and more people are turning to hypnosis, and marathon running, bicycling, ballooning, and other sports that lift one above and beyond the normal parameters of mind, emotions, and body.

It has been indisputably proven that there is a direct connection between the perceptive patterns of the researcher and the reality he "proves" with his research. He has an intuitive knowing that it exists and so draws forth that confirmation. Edgar Cayce used to say, "Mind is builder." Another powerful concept is "A child becomes what he is told." We perceive what we think, but we also perceive what we feel! Plants that keel over dead in the house of a person who claims she has no ability to care for them will magically revive at the hands of a person said to have a green thumb. There are many examples of the way a person's perceptive patterns define and produce his or her reality, not just how it actually is, but how the person interprets it to be. This interdependence between observer, object, and the way of observing has been basic knowledge across many doctrines, specifically spiritual ones that utilize these principles to explore truth from a universal level.

When we consider by what methods and through which focus

we perceive reality, we realize how our clothes, living conditions, furniture, vehicle, and family members, not to mention our occupation, place of work, and leisure activities, all define us and how we have defined reality through our material possessions and the physical world. Since as a species we are predominantly visual, images carried to the brain by the optic nerve are imprinted as true and real whether they are something we see external to ourselves or something we see with our inner vision. Every picture we create and hold in our minds has a real energy within our private and personal universe. The consequences of this are thrilling. It means that if we are able to hold in the mind's eye the visual presentation of a state of being or an "imagined" reality, we could create it, because the brain perceives it that way!

The question is, do you want to change your life? What would happen if you admitted the secret hope that you are a wonderful light being, that light originates within you and radiates from you, that you are transfused with light? What if you strongly visualized yourself as bathed in a glow of soft, shimmering, golden or silver or white or violet light?

Try this. Sit quietly and create such an experience and then simply observe how your vital feelings change when you accept as fact that you are a light being, that you can move as a conscious light being through the world, through life, through birth and death, through many dimensions.

It is my experience that we cannot imagine anything that is not yet a part of our consciousness's repertoire. If, for example, someone experiences an image of being a winged creature able to fly through the skies, or perhaps secretly thinks of herself as being able to heal others through a laying on of her hands, I consider this to be a sign that this person does really—or did, in some previous lifetime—possess these abilities. The original material for these pictures is a part of the person's multidimensional consciousness. These pictures are reflections of one's own experiences from previous lives, other times, different octaves of beingness.

We can learn to draw upon them now; there is no question but that they can be used to alter our reality and expand our capacities in this life.

✔   *Effective Imagination*   ✔

When people first begin to perceive inner visions, they often worry that it is only their "imagination." In our culture we are taught very diligently not to lie. Therefore if we cannot prove something, we feel that we might somehow be punished because the emotional body still lives the threats of childhood in an ever-present now. However, it is fascinating to ponder from whence comes imagination. From the perspective of the Light Institute, we can only create visions out of what is stored within our own multidimensional repertoire. If it is stored there, it is ultimately real for us on some level. Truth is only what we experience. The Higher Self will steer us to movies, for example, that have a frame of reference or association to our multiincarnational, emotional body, which will then react from its own experience to coalesce meaning from the pictures. Nothing happens outside ourselves that is not reflected inside ourselves. What does this imply about our fascination with violent horror movies and the wars and conflicts going on around the world? Are we creating them as they create us?

If we permit ourselves creative visualizations of a positive nature emanating from our spiritual body, energy flows into us, we become more awake, more conscious, and more clear. We can use these inner images to lend our lives a more profound and expanded meaning, a larger dimension. The emotional body, too, is influenced by our conscious awareness of inner vision. It receives new patterns of a higher vibration. We open ourselves to participation with the millions of souls who have participated in creative activities over the aeons and create a bridge to the expression of our own humanity, and are thus able to transcend the power of the emotional or astral body. In most people the emotional body, being highly reactive and easily controlled by negation, mockery, and derision, is able to hinder or distort the manifestation of the creative energies with its slow, dark, sticky, and negative vibrations, which quickly tune in to and are enhanced by the negative vibrations of others. On the emotional octave we have stored our fear and so can easily tap into the fear of all beings on the planet. We are afraid to turn loose into octaves in which the ego streams outward without defensive, self-protective shields that have become our self-identification.

The goal in working with creative imagery is to see directly some of the aspects of our life's plan—the plan each of us formulated before incarnating on this earth. What is it we know, what can we do, what can we give and contribute?

One of the ways to begin to realize and attain this goal is to get in touch with the child within. It is easy and simple to do.

Directing your attention inward, create a safe, quiet space where you will not be disturbed by unwelcome noises and negative-minded people. Loosen your clothing and place your body in a comfortable position. Enter into simple meditation and ask your inner self to remember some time during your childhood when you felt free, elated, full of joy and open and your imagination flowed unhindered. Perhaps at that time you felt the presence of other beings or some communion with animals; maybe you were playing outside or making someone feel happy or well. Seek within you for moments of merging, success, peace, and divine connection. Re-create for yourself these peak experiences and the feelings that accompanied them.

As you move through these experiences, you will find that you can re-create the child within you, the feelings of elation and freedom, the joy and the openness. Now focus your attention on your hopes, intentions, and ideals, the talents and gifts you felt within yourself as a child, those clear moments of certainty, the instant recognitions of camaraderie and the sweet moments when you lost your sense of separateness and felt merged with a place or another being.

All of these spaces reside within you and are accessible to you at any time. You can connect these feelings with your present activities and use them as a light or beacon to direct you into new activities and to direct you away from activities that are not contributing to your purpose in this lifetime. It is important for you to continue to seek those gifts with which you were born so that you can truly live by them. Spiritual orientation is our birthright. Seeking the child within is one of the best ways we have of doing this.

✔ *The Adventure of Living* ❧

New adventures await us within both inner and outer spaces. Discovering new outer and inner space is becoming a mass movement, an evolutionary movement. Humanity cannot survive under the present circumstances of limitation and, in some cases, retrogressive development of consciousness. We must move into new spaces. As we do, as we make new discoveries, our reality changes. Sometimes this is for the better, sometimes for the worse. Progress as we know it is a double-edged sword, particularly with regard to the terrible monster we have unleashed with nuclear radiation half-life periods of twenty to fifty thousand years, over which we have lost control. We are like the sorcerer's apprentices who now have to either execute a quantum leap in the development of our consciousness or else make the retroactive discovery that we have annihilated ourselves.

Beyond the Trojan horse of atomic development lies another Pandora's box of probable horrors: genetic research. Nature produces new mutations, either in an evolutionary or an abrupt way. But whole species on the planet have been lost when the radioactivity we send into the atmosphere has influenced the forms of life on earth. We humans will be no exception. Humanity now feels itself prominent enough to join nature in the game of genetic manipulation. From a karmic perspective, most research on the manipulation of genes is fed by memories from other times, such as in Atlantis, when the Atlantians manipulated the genetic codes and divided the androgynous body into male and female. This division led to ego games that soon became deadly serious: the battle of the sexes, repression, and power struggles, which then extended the theme of polarity to include all beings and nations outside the self. The experience of separation became paramount.

A parallel exists here and now to Atlantis. There, too, people were seduced by the exciting visions and promises of certain experiments, as we are today. Genetic experimentation, babies conceived in petri dishes, mice with human susceptibilities, all managed with shot-in-the-dark rationalizations, have created a many-headed Hydra. We have learned nothing from history because the linear mind cannot grasp all of reality, nor, incidentally, can it alter it. As for ourselves, we became involved with radioactivity once we learned how to split the atom and have thereby constructed a monster that is controlling us, though too few of us realize it as yet. Our only hope, then, is to fully recognize and acknowledge that we may be circling around and repeating history. We must look to higher consciousness to guide us through these precarious explorations, lest we follow the Atlantians to our own demise.

Another of the great adventure spaces, outside of the self, is the contemplation of consciousness on other worlds. Humanity has always hoped and feared that there could be intelligent life on other planets, intelligent beings other than man. Today, many people will admit to being aware that, simply according to the law of probability, there must be intelligent life somewhere among the billions and trillions of suns and their corresponding energy systems.

There is sufficient tangible evidence that we ourselves have been visited by other beings from the outer universe. The potential for these interchanges between ourselves and others from worlds beyond is staggering. That we might transcend the limitations of our present lives is a probable reality we are fast approaching. If we are going to alter our genes, extend our physical horizons, seek and embrace the secrets of the gods, we must give ourselves permission to be who we truly are without fear about how others will judge us. It is necessary for humanity to explore the long held secrets discovered by adepts and hidden from the masses because of desire for personal power and the lack of responsible application of divine laws. In order for the majority to accomplish this, it is crucial that more and more leaders, teachers, and influential people raise their levels of awareness, for with each turnabout in one person's consciousness, there is a corresponding raising of the consciousness of all humanity. The "adventure" is staring us in the face. Let us step forward as fearless beings. From the dimension of the hologram, there is nothing unknown, unwhispered, unforeseen. We can never lose life, we can only be foolish enough to deny it.

Letting the Opponent Win

Every new step of consciousness gains a very personal aspect when it is applied to one's own person, partners, parents, or children. A brief exercise to develop consciousness is, for instance, applauding for the "opposing" team at a sports event, truly feeling and wanting the other team to win. It would be even more effective to do this in a stadium or within a large audience where we really begin to take the part of the "other" team or side. We will notice that we are carried by a wave of energy just as invigorating as is the energy of identification with "our" team. The exercise can easily be expanded and translated in consciousness to the supporting of such divisions as American or Soviet, north or south, Christianity or Islam, various race factors or ideals, chocolate or vanilla—any aspect of one's life where there has developed a polarity or a splitting of alignments.

In doing such an experiment, in dealing with the reflection of the subconscious of groups of people of various magnitudes, we begin to realize our connection to an energy flow. In the matter of games we can feel a certain kind of joy, a peculiar ecstasy, a sense of camaraderie and belonging. It is not so much an identification on a purely factual basis with one or the other side, one or the other theme or attitude; it is the rush of self-identification we seek.

Through the process of what is sometimes called "walking in the other person's moccasins," we can extend the exercise to more personal encounters, including relationships, family situations, disagreements, and misunderstandings. Often, in this process, our positionality will dissolve on its own once we have identified the position of the other person and acknowledged its validity under the circumstances. Our positions, roles, judgments, prejudices, and self-righteousness dissolve the moment we realize that we can identify with the other point of view just as legitimately and with just as much truth as we did with our own. Indeed, in practicing this exercise we soon come to realize that there need not be two opposing viewpoints in any given situation; in fact, there may be a third or transcendent point from which to view an argument that will suit both sides and solve the quandary.

The small death that our ego suffers during such exercises makes us freer to become enlightened. If we simply give in to these small deaths without resistance, we can experience an easy way to transverse any dilemma, arriving at truth's door by surveying the hologram and realizing that we have the freedom to place ourselves equally at any point along the way. Although we lose our identity by giving up the blue team, for example, since we are now cheering the red team, we can instantaneously grasp, if we remain conscious and awake, that there is an intersecting point of truth above and beyond both the teams.

But the emotional body does not do this so easily. It becomes desperate when something is taken away from it because its identity is invested in projection and reaction to the outside world. If we are to make any changes, we must always give the emotional body something to replace what has been released. This is true whether we are talking about replacing a smoking or eating habit or a lover.

We all are aware of such emotional trade-offs from our experiences with intimate relationships. What may have been sheer ecstasy turns to agony when an altercation occurs. The beloved's mannerisms, once so enchanting, become excruciatingly unendurable, and the once charming voice now grates upon the ears. Where once we floated on air, now we feel submerged, drowned, and beyond hope. Sinking to a low ebb, as we wallow in self-pity because of the rejection of our partner, we feel deserted, unloved, worthless, and abysmal. We harbor thoughts of revenge and retribution for real and imagined wrongs.

However, as soon as a new lover appears on the scene, we feel lively, loved, and useful. We quickly begin to consider the formerly damned separation as lucky and auspicious and possibly even send the former partner good wishes and forgiveness.

Our view of reality, of truth and untruth, is colored by and dependent upon our emotional perspective. Our sense of self is weighed and measured by whether or not others find us desirable. This feeling is embedded within the emotional body, which emanates the conclusion. We must open up the emotional body for higher, purer, and lighter vibrations that do not disintegrate at the first frown from the outside world.

One of our great lessons calls for us to emerge from the illusion that we are here on this planet as small and insignificant beings, always having to fight others for survival. By raising our consciousness, we will cultivate our multidimensionality so that the view of the self expands to include our infinite, divine connection. Nourished by this remembrance, the emotional body can heal itself without a fight. The healing takes place, not necessarily by dealing directly with the specific wounds, but by experiencing joy and the higher emotional octaves that allow us to let go and continue on. Since negative and positive repulse each other, by choosing forgiveness and freedom, the wounds are healed without returning to the scenes that induced them.

When I speak of consciousness, I am not speaking of the confines of intellect or reason, I am speaking of holographic perception wherein the resonant wave of knowing echoes out to include all corresponding particles. In our growing and cleansing process, such a simple exercise in consciousness as acquiring a new and different point of view—the view from the perspective of a former "opponent," even on a temporary and experimental basis—can be immensely helpful.

When I speak of emotions and feelings, I am not speaking of ultimate reality, though feelings may appear to be so. Feelings are just as much of an illusion as is time. Both the illusion of time and the illusion of feeling can be oppressive. Happily, when we recognize them as illusion, the experience can be liberating.

✔   *Transcending Feeling*   ↘

Let us simply imagine what would happen if we left out our feelings. This is, for many people, a terrifying prospect because so many of us have come to identify ourselves through the feeling threshold. We determine if things are good or bad, safe or dangerous, by using the emotional body to describe the world from a feeling perspective. As a reality check, this practice is fairly shaky because feelings are so easily wielded by the ego. It is an insidious decoy of the crafty emotional body to pretend that our feelings are a deep part of us when, in fact, feelings are only the outer crust of the emotional body.

Frequently people come to the Light Institute who are very emotionally oriented, very sensitive and vulnerable. Even though this sensitivity has often caused them discomfort or pain, they take pride in it, for they feel it makes them better than others, and they are unwilling to let go of what they consider to be their distinguishing characteristic.

Much to their shock, they often discover, during the sessions, that the source of their being is a different reality or plane where there is no emotional body defined by a feeling component as they know it now. They realize that the theme of their incarnation on earth is to make the acquaintance of emotions, to deal with polarities, and to combine and merge opposites. Through developing the heart vibrations, they will grow in comprehension to a new

octave of love as a natural quality of their multidimensional consciousness. These are galactic beings, beings from the depths of
the universe, who have come here to this planet in order to
experience and learn certain lessons related to emotional reality.
One interesting aspect of this discovery is that they try so hard
to become and appear human that they overamplify and exaggerate
the feelings they try so hard to acquire. In their efforts to be
accepted, they overcompensate for their lack of knowledge of the
local emotional language. Though all of this drama and masking
is subconscious, such people want to ensure that they appear
normal, especially to themselves.

Our intergalactic visitors want to ensure, equally at all cost,
that everyone around them believes them to be human, so they
make a show of their feelings, they dramatize and wallow in them.
Then one day they discover they were actually only playing with
human feelings here, just as we sometimes cheer with all our hearts
and energies for our team; but no matter to what level we raise
our projection and loyalty, we are not the team. So, too, we have
feelings, but we are not feelings.

In this respect feelings are an illusion and a huge cosmic joke.
Once we have experienced the possibility that we use them as
connecting devices to create ties with others, we can transcend
them by using the heart as the point of melding. Thus we can free
ourselves of all emotional patterns related to the game of survival.
We can remove our masks and see ourselves in the mirror for
who we truly are.

We have other things to learn from these galactic beings. Usually
they have not consciously had anything to do with metaphysics,
esoteric questions, or the possibility of extraterrestrial experience.
Yet at the Light Institute they discover and experience for themselves that they are of galactic origin. They have clear and detailed
experiences that they describe to us. They tell of wonderful space
stations and a network of research laboratories, the purpose of
which is to transplant newly created genetic material as "seeds"
on various planets in diverse galaxies, in order to study the evo-

lution of life forms based on varying genetic information. The words they speak, the experiences they describe, are totally unlike any they were aware of before they opened up their consciousness. These are direct and valid experiences, directed by the Higher Self. Our role is nothing more than to create a safe space for them to open up to this growth and new awareness.

How do we explain it? Beyond the fact that some things just are not explainable, I feel this is a sign that some myths of creation may well be true. One of these myths, persistent in many cultures, is that an extraterrestrial intelligence (superior or higher beings) may have initiated the creation or evolution of life on this planet and others. These beings have been interpreted as God or angels or other beings descending from Heaven or Olympus or from a sea or airgoing vessel of some kind in order to create life on earth, in order to breathe life into humankind. Another interpretation is that gods or divine emissaries entered into physical union with humans in order to create a new race of humanity.

When we view this with the eyes of the linear or left half of the brain, we cannot comprehend the wholeness of a being who exceeds the individual form, as we see it. The linear brain deals only with intellectual analogies and the limitation of assumed time and space boundaries.

But when we become the child within, we return to the use of both sides of our brain, and, further, we delve into our genetic consciousness where knowledge of and participation in extraterrestrial dimensions pulsates as it circulates within our blood crystals. This planet desperately needs all the wisdom of the universe to resolve our present dilemmas. Open your consciousness to the possibilities that this conversation has raised and look within yourself for verification of the truth of which I speak. Extraterrestrial beings may seem a bit more alien to you than do trees, plants, animals, insects, and others, but they are nonetheless part and parcel of the divine energy. We are not made less divine when we become open to all other forms in which divine energy is expressed.

✍ *Being a Woman, a Man, a Human Being* ✎

While we are in the process of adopting a new frame of reference
for the world, we begin to reexamine our own self-identification
in terms of all the restrictive thought forms and conditions we
have placed on our creative expression. One of the most outmoded
categories of expression is that of gender. To be a woman or a
man as these roles are presently defined is a far too limiting concept
when placed up against a cosmic backdrop. Our multiincarnational
repertoire includes a vast array of possibilities beyond specific
gender. Androgyny, multiphase bodies, light bodies, are just a few
of the magnificent expressions we have known on other planes of
life. Being a man or a woman can be a source of great confusion
and a burden to many people, particularly as our parameters have
become expanded in recent years and we no longer have the specific
roles to play that once were so crystallized and definite.

A person may have a physical body that is male in gender yet
is endeavoring in every way to continue the opposite sexual identity
because of a bleeding over from a previous lifetime. If an earlier
experience was very profound for the soul, allowing it to soar to
new heights facilitated by the orientation of the body, or the
emotional body met with a heart-wrenching disaster due to the
form of the body, then there may be a freeze, a fixation wherein
the emotional body simply does not acknowledge any new reality
and will seek to continue what it was experiencing. It is a confusing and terrible experience to feel more comfortable with the
behaviors and surroundings of the opposite gender when we don't
have a clue as to the reason.

Then, too, the wishes and proclivities of parents tend to play
an important part in our attitudes toward our sexual gender. If
only parents could become aware that their small embryo is listening by loudspeaker to their every thought and statement about
what they need and want from the child to be. Statements like
"We hope so much it will be a boy to carry on the family name,"
or "I only want a girl. I wouldn't know what to do with a boy,"

are profound influences on the self-image of the child. The world is full of "tomboys" trying desperately to hit the hammer with the nail, agonizingly hoping for a glimmer of recognition from their father that often is not forthcoming. A girl whose parents wished for a boy throughout the pregnancy and her early childhood may drag around with her, all her life, the emotional patterns and imprints that were caused by the tension between her parents' desire and her own life plan. In such instances, as in other conflicts, we are constantly nudged toward examining closely how and why we chose our life situation, problems, and traumas. By opening up to the divine energy of our Higher Self and by letting our Higher Self lead us back to the dimensions of causes, origins, and responsibility, we can divest ourselves of our unconscious embedding in such patterns, and on this plane as well as the higher planes, we can break through the vicious cycle.

When we are in the spiritual or even the astral body, when we go on journeys into higher dimensions, it becomes fairly irrelevant whether or not we occupy a male or female body here on earth. Likewise, before we enter the threshold of puberty, we are graced with more freedom from exclusively male or female behavior requirements. Thus the tomboy climbs happily in the trees or beats the neighboring boys at running games, while the little boy who loves gentle music is allowed to dress up in his mother's clothes and spends his time listening to the women conversing about emotional dramas.

Once these children reach puberty, the door slams shut and they are abandoned to the whim of their hormones with little or no explanation from their parents as to what is happening, just an ever-tightening loop of demands and behavior modeling as to what is a male or a female. These experiences of puberty are strong and imprint forcefully on the emotional body; they remain in effect throughout the following decades or even our entire life. So these adolescents will distrust themselves and their environments because of the changes they went through and the concomitant turmoil. Among other things, the integrity of their self-image was shaken.

However, if we are introduced to concepts of expanding the consciousness at an early age, all the gifts and talents accrued from bodies of each (and both) gender can merge and provide us with a rich human emotional repertoire. Thus the girl can live within her emerging femininity and still participate actively in masculine expression, while the boy can permit himself full emotional openness, synchronistic to male modes of expression.

✍ *Balancing Male and Female Energies* ❧

In order to bring balance and harmony to this seemingly irreconcilable polarity of male/female expression, we must learn to live both kinds of energies equally. The Higher Self will help us by exposing us to the akashic records that hold our souls' memory of bodily experience so that we can clear away old thought forms of familial, cultural bias as to the preferred value and expression of each.

At the Light Institute we uncover not only the male and female incarnations we have experienced, but all the genetic coding of true yin and yang energies. Through this process, we experience directly that just as the body carries the physical DNA to design its form, there are emotional and spiritual DNA that piggyback into the third dimension as well. The tree of inheritance holds the future and the past, which are both modified by the present. We must access all men within us, all women, all mothers and fathers, all children, so as to attain a balancing of yin and yang energies and create a new species.

If, for instance, we are inhabiting a male body, we must also explore all the different female aspects of ourselves. If we experience the loving woman, the maternal aspect, the creative female energy, the wise priestess, and the little girl within ourselves, we will be free to merge with a woman, as a man, in such a way as to produce a harmonious fusion. This is, of course, true in the reverse as well, for souls that are now in a female body. Only when we have found, as a woman, the male energy within us—

the father, the warrior, the little boy, the focus of the priest, and all other aspects of yang energy—will we be able to communicate and fuse with the male energy outside.

We can enter into a relationship without projections, without emotional blocks, only when we have been through these inner experiences. Then we know from exploring our own emotional repertoire how to relate to the energies that are expressed in the person of the opposite sex.

One of our greatest sources of fear is our unconscious knowledge of the "unspeakable" within us, such as the suspicion that we have energies from which we are alienated, or disconnected, but which we sense are wielding their influence upon us. If we live in a male body and also possess a repertoire of female feelings, thoughts, and conduct patterns that are guarded and veiled, we may not be able to separate these totally normal energies from other, more blatant misuses of our power that have been the tools of the soul's growth. Guilt is the most destructive of energies that so misinterprets the divine purpose in every and all experience.

The future of partnership and relationship is blissful fusion, peacefully awaiting our enlightenment. Knowledge of the self is the key. The self does not produce judgment and blame as the poor emotional body would have us believe; it is filled with the light of compassion and the radiance of the human heart that we all came here to experience.

The Earth Lives

Planet Earth is a living, conscious being. People who meditate or have otherwise developed their awareness can experience the nature of a tree in a direct way, talk to plants, become a flower or a cliff. Not only does this enrich our earthly experience, but it can and will become very crucial to our survival in the near future.

We must begin to experience that we are a living part of this world and that the earth itself is a mirror, an echo of our collective consciousness. The earth lives; gases, minerals, water, fire, air—

all these elements are also within our own bodies. The belief that matter has no consciousness is one of the great illusions of humanity, along with the illusion of time, our emotions, our origins. Everything that becomes matter possesses consciousness. A flower possesses consciousness, the sea is conscious, the wind, too. Ancient human cultures always communed with nature to protect the balance of all life. "Modern" man with his linear ways prefers to smile at these facts. However, since we have no technological solutions to help us deal with the consequences of the monsters of radioactivity, oil spills, and toxic wastes, we will have to reenter dialogue with the earth, who may be contemplating our demise at this very moment due to our refusal to communicate. In the grand scheme of things, it is we who might be considered a pestilence to the rest of life.

Everything that possesses form contains consciousness. We can learn from this consciousness, which is the matrix, the glue of form itself. The earth is cosmic, conscious life, and we are part of its substance and outer skin. The earth itself is within the medium of a great universe in which it participates in the cosmic flow. It relates to other celestial bodies, other cells of the great universe. We have decided, for a multitude of reasons, to develop on the surface of this terrestrial cell. To the degree to which we perceive our universal energies, our symbiotic life, with and upon the earth, we shall also be able to feel how other celestial bodies, such as Jupiter and Saturn, say, are also conscious beings. It is odd to observe how some people want to limit life according to conditions they consider valid. According to them, life develops and can exist only in this or that temperature range, only when certain elements are present, only when a specific force of gravity reigns. Who says, though, that *life* and *conscious being* follow the limits of thought and confines of perception compatible only to our physical spectrum of reality?

Thousands of people report conscious life experiences on multitudinous planets outside the range stipulated by our present understanding. There are enough indications experienced in states of profound meditation, in great ecstasy, in journeys of the consciousness into other dimensions, that the other physical and nonphysical dimensions are filled with creative energy and intelligence.

Whole worlds of new knowledge through higher mind await us if we can again become the child and set ourselves free to explore. While it is true that new approaches have always been accompanied by immense resistance and hostility, this is precisely why we must clear the emotional body of its fears and hunger for acceptance. The great cannot wait for the small to confirm what is true. Discovery is a gift we each give to ourselves; that is its true purpose. Thus Newton went beyond the Middle Ages, Einstein beyond Newton, and we are moving beyond Einstein. We don't have to ask permission, we just have to want to, from the point of light of the Fearless Self!

✔   *Communication with the Animal World*   ➤

It is well known that a relationship with animals provides a very effective instrument for healing the emotions. Sometimes we suffer extreme feelings of separation from others, but by establishing a conscious contact with other forms of life we can experience a decisive opening up of our heart and a newly stimulated energy flow. A person can forget human limitations and isolation while in a relationship with an intelligent, caring animal. When we focus on a tree, a plant, a bird, or other animals such as horses, dogs, cats, and the many varied pets people choose, the language we speak with them is the language of the heart—that is, the universal means by which all forms of consciousness can communicate with each other. The benefits of human/animal relationships have been proven by experiments with humans and animals made in children's hospitals and in prisons. Children who are given the opportunity of being and playing with young animals recover much faster than other children. Prison inmates, especially men, who are allowed to care for an animal become much less aggressive and depressed than other inmates.

Situations where animals are trained to make a contribution have long resulted in the development of effective partnerships such as those between police officers and their dogs, trackers and bloodhounds, the blind person and his Seeing Eye dog. The interdependence of hunters and their hounds, shepherds, sheep, and dogs, beekeepers and bees, all demonstrate the many varied ways the animal kingdom and humanity can develop symbiotic relationships. These creatures and their "masters" have always been able to communicate, and each member of the relationship affects and is affected by the other.

Experiments have been done with dolphins, apes, and monkeys in order to investigate to what extent we can converse with them, using symbols for words. It remains doubtful what sense it makes to measure intelligence and the capacity for communication according to whether or not other species can comprehend and converse in our language. Perhaps it would make more sense if we tried to learn the animals' means of communication, on a holographic octave.

Let me tell you the story of my St. Bernard dog and his gallant effort to communicate with me after his death. We were leaving for Bolivia and made the difficult decision to leave him behind, as I knew the Bolivians would find him a bit scary. The week before we left, he suddenly disappeared. After the second day I became very concerned for him and began to meditate and call to him psychically. That night I was startled awake about three A.M. by a huge infrared cloud that came in through the window. As I stared in terror at the cloud, it formed itself into the shape of my dog, lingered a few seconds, and disappeared. I knew that my beloved dog had used all his power to reach across the dimensions of space to release me. The next day I took my pendulum out onto the eighty-thousand-acre ranch behind the house and, after two hours, found his body. The man who shot him was so sure that no one would find him in such a huge area that he had simply driven him off in his truck and, removing his tags, dumped him in a small arroyo. I felt that he had chosen death for my sake, but his power to communicate with me in that way links him to me as one of my greatest teachers in this lifetime.

Another powerful example of this lies within a story my Higher Self told me to tell in this book as an example of how thoughts and feelings become manifest. Again, the lesson is a painful one for me and has become a guardian to my thoughts, lest I ever indulge desire again.

Since childhood I have been fascinated with everything Indian (Native American): Indian art, crafts, culture. I have since learned that I have lived many powerful Indian lifetimes, and I have been able to release myself from these patterns. At that time, however, I was still simply enthralled by Indian artifacts without being consciously aware of the basis for my fascination.

One day, when I went to a small Indian store in Santa Fe, I spotted the most beautiful bobcat pelt I had ever seen. I stroked the fur, delighted in the large paws and the dark spots in the ocher-colored belly of the pelt. I wanted to buy it. On the other hand, it was important to me not to help create a market that would perpetuate the killing of these wonderful animals, as there are not many bobcats left in the mesas of New Mexico. Consequently I left the store without buying the pelt.

Three days later I was riding with another person, in a large Dodge van, when I saw something like a large animal crossing the highway. I noticed it hide itself in the shrubs on the meridian. Strangely enough, just as we were passing the animal's hideout, it purposefully jumped directly in front of the car and was caught by the wheels. We stopped, went back, and found a large, beautifully marked bobcat in the last throes of death. At this moment I experienced a feeling of recognition and sensed the same coming from the bobcat's eyes. I had had a great desire to have a bobcat pelt but had not wanted to be responsible in a direct or an indirect way for the death of any animal. Now this bobcat had caused its own death by intentionally and in full consciousness throwing itself under the wheels of my car.

I took the bobcat into my arms and was caught up in a wave

of direct communion between human being and animal. This taught
me, beyond any intellectual knowing, that communication between
the species takes place, not only on auditory and emotional octaves,
but also on the spiritual octave.

That bobcat had, on some octave of his multidimensional being,
perceived my wish. Within him was the awareness that death is
not the end, so he gave his life to teach me about the power of
desire. This experience was another turning point in my life, since
I experienced in a direct way that we are not separated from each
other. I will never forget a single one of the myriad sensations
that flooded my very being when I held that "wild animal" in my
own arms and felt his fur, looked into his great eyes, and felt the
last surge of energy course through him as his spirit lifted up from
his body.

Within the higher dimensions, not only are we not separated
from parents, partners, children, and all persons in our surroundings, we are also not separated from nature and the other species
on this planet. The lesson of the bobcat was a drastic one. Immediately after the incident I felt sorrow and grief because of my
responsibility for having caused the death of this beautiful animal,
my brother, although I knew he had chosen this synchronicity to
make a breakthrough with a human spirit. Through me, he will
always live.

✦   *Change: The Soul of Creative Energy*   ➤

If there is one chant in the universe, it is to *create*. Everything that
lives seeks to participate in the cosmic splendor of variation of the
theme, the form, the energy of life itself. Change is the propagator
of variation, breathing life into every design by opening the spin
point, the threshold, to whatever might be beyond, either by
memory or by germination.

We must open ourselves upward and inward in order to grow.
It is as though an arrow pierces our heart. If we close ourselves,
the arrow can become a festering wound, yet if we open, healing

energy can flow freely and we will come out of the experience stronger, more powerful, and with an intangible aura of greater stature through having successfully met a challenge. If our lives are based on action, not reaction, we can dare to open, expand, and extend the best we have to offer, for the sake of our own souls. "Where there is no resistance, there is no harm!"

In the case of creating a book, for example, we need to relinquish endeavoring to totally control from the outside and to seek within for the purpose and direction of the experience. The creative process forces us to give up control as the created entity, whether a baby, a book, a painting, or an invention, begins to dictate its own needs as it takes shape. Often you will hear a carpenter say, "A nail wants to go here," or a painter will speak of a color that "needs" to go in a certain place. Sometimes the process of relinquishing control involves a state of utter chaos, total disorder, "till no stone is left unturned," so that the old barriers and mental barricades are totally dissolved, and new states of being are created on the ashes of the disarray.

Often it is only when we give up ego control that the unmanifest can come forth and be manifest in a new, more beautiful, miraculous, and enlightened way. At the center of this spiritual and physical development are the spheres of joy, happiness, and ecstasy. Sometimes, to contact these states, we go through opposite states, and the process can be excruciatingly painful. Resistance is always what causes the pain, not change, which whispers encouragement through its powerful gift of energy. No one sleeps through change!

The message of the energy spiral is that we are indestructible. We are part of a great cosmic orchestra, and we will enjoy our playing more if we consciously learn to recognize our role, our function, and our purpose within the whole.

Within the Emotional Triangle

The Magic Triangle

The essential shape of our emotional world is the triangle. Within its confines are all the functional and instructional elements that create the form of relationships throughout our entire journey of a lifetime. The cornerstones of this magical configuration are the parent, child, and partner, who complete a hologram capable of myriad intersecting energies of fusion. The parents fuse to bring forth the child, who rushes headlong into the partner, with whom the process begins anew. It is an unending pulse of intimate, karmic attraction in which the three points mix and merge until the emotional body has come to recognize how each is within the one, and the one is present in the all.

Everything we learn about ourselves through relationship comes from this triad. Even in business and other such formal relationships, we tend unconsciously to decide which of the three primary roles best suits us and maneuver the underlying design to fit it. Thus we might have the secretary who keeps the office going by playing the mother or the successful executive whose faithful employees jump to his command because he conveys the protective security of the father. Each position in the triangle has certain specific characteristics that define and limit expression from within it.

If we want to heal and clear our emotional body, we must not overlook uncovering the clandestine aspects represented by any of the three corners of our triangle. In one instance we are in a relationship where we are the children and the relevant others are the parents; in another we are the parents and the others the children; and in the third instance the relevant others are our partners. We can know the child in us while we are actually children, sense the child in us even when we are with our partner, and also in relationship to our own children. In the same vein we can feel that we are partners of our children, our parents, and our partners.

The effect of stimulating this energy flow is that the pyramid or triangle of three-dimensionality becomes transformed into the spiritual spiral, as the energy progresses from corner to corner and begins to spin upward. All too frequently, though, we get stuck in one corner of the triangle or block ourselves up in it: I am a parent, I am a man or woman, I am a child. The corners represent potential transitions or turning points between the various facets of our capacity to relate. They are the points of merger or fusion that act as thresholds to higher dimensional relationship potential. If we are consciously present in all the corners and experience all the various facets of our relating capacities to an equal degree, we activate the energy spiral, which is accessible to us through the focal points. Initially it may be hard to imagine what this could mean to us because the repertoire of relationship on this planet is so stilted.

Accessing the parent frequency, for example, opens up the creative flow in which we can become the source of new energy. Instead of projecting that the child has all the energy, if we experience ourselves as the fountain from which new growth, new thought, and new life flows, we begin to be the partners of divine manifestation. Most of the emotional imbalances of today's world stem from this inability to utilize energy. The results are depression, denial, and inertia.

It does not matter whether we address the external or the internal parent, child, or partner. The inner balancing of energies from the different aspects of our being is the condition, the prerequisite, for clearing external relationships. At the same time, this inner balancing of energies is conducive to our attaining higher, spiritual dimensions that offer us the clarity to comprehend the whys and hows of the living triads.

✔ *Karmic Bonds* ✔

Relationships seem plagued by karmic bonds left over from other scenarios and the triad configuration. The attracting mechanisms that pull us into relationships are definitely infused with illusion, projection, and manipulation.

Whenever we feel a strong desire for someone, we should investigate what karmic theme is at the root. If we develop an incredibly passionate, powerful feeling for someone who seems to attract us magnetically, we are staring karma straight in the face! This is definitely true of "love at first sight." We must begin by investigating the sources of this attraction and what part we want to give this person in the theater of our life. Is it sex appeal? Do we believe that person to be our soul-mate? Is it recognition of a person from the same genetic "soul community" as are we? Perhaps we only feel attracted to someone because the two of us had a mother-son relationship in our former lives. Frequently, when a person thinks, "This must be my soul-mate," it turns out to be karmic bonds on the emotional body's octave rather than the presumed spiritual connection of divine energies. Of course, our soul-mates are the ones who help us with our karmic lessons of cause and effect; it's just that we create that to be painful because we have so little understanding of the process.

Mutual sexual, erotic attraction is one of the main hooks for relationships. Multiincarnatonal explorations reveal fascinating convolutions on this theme of the emotional triangle. Leftover passions from other lives create tremendous confusion in this life when they are not appropriate or conscious; witness the physical discomfort between parent and teenager that Freud termed Oedipal. We would view this from the vantage point of many lifetimes spent together in alternating triangular roles of partners, parents, and children. The karmic reality is not misplaced here since our sexual energy is closest to the spiritual creative energies. Through sexual energy, the divine spark enters into a new form, a new life, from the unmanifest.

On the other hand, it also makes sense to check whether there is, in truth, a purely spiritual relationship of empathy that can express itself through an exchange of energies of the higher chakras or whether we are being drawn into an energy exchange of the lower chakras, specifically the navel and the sexual centers, from sheer habit and old memories that would serve our evolution to transmute onto another octave.

Is the partner a reflection of ourselves? Is he the projection of our wishes, longings, and fantasies? The most successful relationships are those in which both partners have explored and recognized the source, the divine purpose, for their having met. Both need to know who they are independently of the other, here on earth and in the multidimensional realities. Also, both need to know who they become together, so as not to be tempted to repeat behavioral patterns from relationships that bound them in other lives and other dimensions. They must know of each other what they have already finished successfully, and it is, incidentally, a most exciting adventure to recognize this! Now they are free to fuse with one another in a new way, to open up new octaves together that they might never attain separately.

The best partnership is not dominated by emotional patterns, by karmic vicious circles that limit the direction and development of the relationship. There have been but few ideal relationships on this earth because we have strange thought forms about how we must create ties to bind us. Bondage never amplifies love. Cosmic truth demonstrates that we are never separate, but we must work to clear away the veils in order to experience this. We expect the other person to take care of us; the other person expects the same from us; and thus we create a self-devouring relationship. This is a relationship that sucks away and uses up our energies. An ideal relationship creates a channel for new energy that stems from a profound and enlightened exchange between two people. Fusion, or merging of two human beings, creates a vibration that resounds in the world around them. Instead of being concerned exclusively with one another and fading away, such a relationship is a gift for the surrounding world. An outward-directed energy spiral emerges and lets the creative, loving vibrations flow outward.

✔ Healing Ourselves Through the World Around Us ✎

One magical layer of the emotional triangle is the self, the world, and the Higher Self. We can use the world to echo the themes we ourselves are working on and employ the Higher Self as the grand initiator that keeps the energy flowing in order to stimulate awareness.

As soon as the Higher Self reveals itself to us in some form and we receive it within our bodies, we begin the transformation of surrender to this divine energy. It does not imply blind surrender such as often happens toward exterior authority. It is, instead, an intimate connection to our own creative powers. A marvelous game ensues in which the Higher Self employs the outside world, placing people and situations squarely in our path so that we can use them to discover and heal ourselves. If, for instance, we inhabit a male body, we can ask our Higher Self to reveal itself as our own female energies. The consequences are very far reaching. Perhaps we are speaking to our landlady soon afterward and realize that she speaks the way we think. Suddenly we feel a bond of trust with her. Ultimately we will be able to see in every person around us the reflection of some aspect of ourselves. Instead of developing negative reactions, we will find not only the mirror of the outer self, but the reflection of the Higher Self in everyone we meet.

If we view everything as a mirror of ourselves, we can learn a lot about what is going on beneath the surface of our emotional body. This premise is almost too overwhelming for the linear mind: *we create our own reality.* If the concept of that much power is inconceivable to us, perhaps we can start with a softer yet no less catalytic reality: "We are a part of everything, everything is a part of us!"

It is fascinating to become involved in the synchronicity of events in the universe. To experience firsthand that our world is a stage, that we play our drama on this stage, and that we create everything and everyone in our life can be wondrous fun. Let us say we see a little girl crying outside. We can explore how she represents the little girl crying within us, and by contacting the child within, we can experience a healing that we ourselves have created. Our Higher Self will delightfully produce another little girl who is laughing and playing happily to signal to us that a transformation has occurred.

This is a wonderful way to play with reality, by perceiving the world around us as an instrument of confirmation we can use to guide our path. The world around us is not, after all, separate or detached from us. Every being we see on the street, every life situation we perceive outside of ourselves, is within us. Instead of resisting this, we simply need to let our consciousness expand so far that we can try out this way of viewing things. The power lies in healing internal energies and seeing their transmutation reflected in the world.

It is exciting to say, "I will not ignore that. Instead, I will focus on it and transform this disharmony into a state of light. I will live in the here and now, I will accept my responsibility and give my gift." We hereby enter into dimensions of consciousness that are filled with ecstasy.

One of the most fundamental human longings is to belong, to count, to be able to contribute something. By becoming involved with our world in this fashion, we can establish a completely new kind of contact with the universal unconscious. This inevitably fills us with joy. We begin the divine exercises of radiance!

Healing one's own emotions and healing the universe's "emotions" are reciprocal processes. We are every tree, every being, every star. We consist of the same elements and share a common destiny. Healing our emotions facilitates lifting the emotional qualities of all human beings to the highest octave. We begin to feel "whole" in a completely new sense when we focus our attention beyond even another person, onto feeling a tree, a dog, the sea, a star, as part of ourselves.

It often happens that the form of the Higher Self, as we perceive it, changes. Again, if we receive this new form into our bodies, it aligns us to yet another window to the sky. It is a constant growth process: re-creating ourselves, creating new worlds, reawakening to our Higher Self. Our spiritual repertoire is purposeful and yet unending.

✦ The Higher Self: The Soul's Megaphone ❧

Once we have established a connection with our Higher Self, we embark upon the most profound initiation of the path to enlightenment. As we learn to surrender and trust, the whole illusion that we must survive begins to crumble, and we experience our first glimpses of the horizon of eternal consciousness. The closer we join with our Higher Self, the farther out into timeless space we move, the farther beyond all boundaries we go. The expansion frees us from the agony of the emotional body caught on the karmic treadmill of birth and death and opens us up to the breathtaking reality that we are eternal. All ancient cultures knew seers and complete systems of wisdom that helped them access beyond the third dimension. They always used the capacity to intentionally focus their inner consciousness in order to bridge the unmanifest and receive guidance from their spiritual energies. What is special about this moment in the universe is that *we* are finally ready to be the participants of divine communication ourselves!

It is as if we are awakening from a long, drugged sleep and must remember that we know the language, that we can speak. What shamans practice, which is erased from childhood, is that this language roots itself in the interface between the physical and nonphysical worlds. We may receive answers through the sudden call of a bird or the song of the wind. The knowing comes in the still of our receptive center, communing with higher consciousness

born to us all, each and every one. Every great culture understood
the wisdom of inner and outer communication between humans,
animals, environment, and nature. Modern man has lost his way
through the choice of automation. He has become disconnected
and inert. As his mind refuses the magic, he has lost touch with
his soul.

The Higher Self is the megaphone of the soul. It amplifies the
ethereal essence and translates it into an expression we can grasp
in material form. It is not a separate being. It is the energy of our
true self. We really only need ask our Higher Self to take form.
Since it is not something separate from us, we needn't struggle;
we need no ritual or complicated formula—just intention, which
is the most powerful tool of manifestation.

This is my recommendation for contacting the Higher Self initially.

*Spin around in a clockwise motion until you feel dizzy. Then sit down,
breathe deeply several times, and ask the Higher Self to make itself visible
to you. Breathe into the nothingness and feel for a presence. It may be
that you will see a bright light or a cloud; some people see colors, some a
shape; there could be a symbol such as a triangle or some strange object.
Whatever shows itself to you represents the energy that will help you open
up your multidimensionality. Do not try to choose for yourself what form
you think is good enough to be your Higher Self. It will change form often
to allow you different access points to the hologram. Simply take the first
impression that comes and focus your attention on it. Begin to draw the
energy radiating from it toward you. It will be very subtle. Don't expect
some overpowering being or force to overwhelm you. The Higher Self takes
the form that will most harmonize and balance your energy at this moment.*

*Pull the form in which the Higher Self presents itself into you, as if you
were inhaling it. Observe at the same time what part of your body receives
this manifestation of the Higher Self. This, too, conveys a message. The
Higher Self might enter through the head, the soles of the feet, or the
heart, through the third eye or the throat. It will be received by us at the
point where we most require energy, in that part of our body that most*

needs higher vibrations. It could also enter us through the channel that is
most healing and through which we are most able to expand.

To bring the Higher Self into resonance with our physical body
in this way allows it to become firmly anchored in this dimension,
on this terrestrial, human octave. Our consciousness expands so
that the lonely emotional body forgets itself as it reaches out to
embrace the higher vibrations of joy and ecstasy.

✒   *New Relationships*   ➹

Our perfect partner is the Higher Self. Though we can't make love
to it or cuddle it in our bed physically, it is still eminently present
to fill us with love. It doesn't ask for breakfast or change its clothes.
It never goes away on business or vacation without us. It never
spends time on the phone or bores us with trivial conversation.

Yet when we turn our attention onto the physical plane, we
forget this divine marriage entirely. If we used it as the standard
for relationship, the quality and wealth of wisdom we could gain
would be immeasurable.

Sadly, the emotional body has a propensity for imprinting the
tragic rather than the ecstatic experiences of relationship and so
dooms itself to repetition. Frequently we can observe that partners
are afraid of entering into a new relationship after a divorce or
separation or that they very quickly fall back into a very similar
relationship, which evokes the same behavioral patterns as the last
one, even choosing partners with similar physical characteristics.
Until we have grasped the source of our life themes, we will either
refrain fearfully from new relationships or continue to be driven
by the emotional blocks and habitual reactions that re-create exactly what we are trying to avoid. This dilemma can be solved by
working on the emotional body through other time and space
dimensions provided by the Higher Self.

Seeing relationships from the perspective of multiincarnations
helps us diminish the amount of projection we place on those

closely associated with us. We invest and project so completely in someone that we are sure that person is the only one we could ever love. The terrible cosmic joke is that the person in question is only *one* bearer among thousands of others of this love projection, which are all distinguished by a similar or identical energy. We focus on certain vibrations that can be intimately connected to our energy according to the patterns of our emotional body. We move from one partner to the next, always working on the same or similar themes, until we finally get to the source themes, often more involuntarily than not. If we can finally free ourselves from a theme, we discover that we can at least find a new point of departure with the next partner. Thereby we start a new chapter, dedicating our energy to the solving of new problems instead of remaining grounded in old karmic ties.

Lurking in our fantasies is the illusion of the soul-mate who will be everything to us, who will make us complete and whole, who will offer us eternal bliss. No one measures up to this ideal, and as a result we miss many opportunities for a powerful relationship, right there in front of us. Bound to the law of energies, we automatically seek that partner who corresponds absolutely to our aura, to our field of energy. Karma makes no errors. Our spiritual family forces us to grow. Accordingly we always find the right members of our spiritual family at the right time to instill the developmental impulses in us.

It is not enough to quit or finish a relationship. It must be transmuted and released on a spiritual level. We cannot continue to resent or harbor anger toward an old partner and hope to establish a new relationship that does not carry the mark of the old.

✔   *Free Relationships*   ✘

Relationships are too often based on a triangle of disaster: you, me, and our respective shadows from past experience. It is a very crowded spacing that offers little freedom of movement, since one or the other of us is always bumping into a shadow and mistaking it for the real person. A truly free relationship in this sense is based on conscious decisions made by both partners. The conscious decision means entering completely into something new without resistance, without fear, without projections and prejudices and using it with grace to create something new.

This is not the self-delusion we sometimes come up with of needing a new partner simply because we happen to be bored. In such cases we imagine that new energy from outside ourselves can help us develop new energy and redefine ourselves. This will not succeed, though, as long as we do not discover who we are, at least in a rudimentary fashion.

When we are in the process of separating from a partner, we are often overcome by anger and fear, those two initial expressions of our emotional body's patterns. That original wound that has never completely healed—the first separation from the divine omniscience—breaks open again in such situations. We simply project it onto a human level, into the event that is our partner leaving us, for instance. We feel lost, betrayed, even worthless. Or we are angry at our partner.

Fear and anger, whether conscious or not, are the primary obstacles in achieving a free relationship. We cannot really love someone if we fear them or are angry at them. This is particularly evident if we feel exhausted after a brief meeting on a sexual, emotional, or mental plane because we could not develop new creative energy, because we were stuck in old energy blocks. As long as we live in fear of losing a person, it is clear that we have not yet found ourselves. Our inner source is truly eternal; there is nothing we can lose. If we recognize ourselves, we experience that we create our own relationships in order to grow through them. We ourselves can decide whether we want a relationship that will end in mutual or unilateral rejection or what course of dramatic events we want to choose.

To be free, we have to give freedom as well. Radiating unconditional love, we transcend the bondage of projection that so limits expression. Freedom does not imply transgression of agreements or commitments to others, it simply expands the arch of consciousness that opens the avenues to the self. Sometimes the greatest demonstration of love is to free someone in a relationship so that they can grow in ways that perhaps are not compatible to our own at that moment. The love never stops, only the necessity to accompany each other in body. As we become aware of our potential to love each other from the octaves of spirit, we can redefine the entire experience of divorce or separation to be a loving gift, such as the parent gives the child who must grow up and leave the nest, albeit not the family.

Family, Divorce, Separation

All families share certain genetic and psychic patterns. The child developed from the mixture of genetic potential of both parents. Inherent emotional imprints are passed down through the intricate strands of physical as well as emotional DNA. Thus the child has immediate and direct psychic and spiritual access to the most profound emotional currents of both parents. Neither father nor mother can, for instance, hide their fear and anxiety from the child. The energies and emotional processes of the parents are experienced in a direct manner. The child interacts with both auric fields and feels what happens when the auras of the parents meet, so the child knows from the beginning about the process of the parents' relationship. Since small children are oblivious to behavioral masks, they rely specifically on the energies they intuit by perceiving parental exchanges that take place behind the external emotional cloaking devices.

The parents model their relationship patterns to the child, who imprints them as an integral part of the soul lessons he or she has selected for growth on a soul level. Though we resist the idea that we choose our parents, we do choose them for our "highest good." So often our cognition of this takes years, even decades, to discover.

C. G. Jung formulated it thus: "Ask a man what he thinks of

his mother, and he will show you how he treats his wife." It is of utmost importance that we realize that the child already knows what developments within the family are necessary and helpful for his own existence. As with all other relationships, the central issues in family relationships are the exchange of energies and energetic processes. It makes no difference whether the parents have never fought in front of the children or have never raised their voices. If the parents are in disharmony, the child knows this. The child not only feels this vibration, he uses it for his own development.

Today, even in very traditional societies, we can observe more and more separations between spouses in relationships that were expected to last forever. Divorce is an important topic of discussion around the world. This trend is neither coincidence nor tragedy, but merely an expression of the quickening of growth necessary for each soul to take its place as an intentional being on the planet. This means that the dissolution of long-standing relationships is not the cause of problems, but rather the concomitant symptom of a change of consciousness. Without the crutch of traditional roles, each being must access inner resources of both male and female energies to deal with the multitudinous demands of daily existence. In so doing, we discover hidden strengths and faculties we would normally project onto and demand from our partner, whom we often criticize for not doing the task as well as we might ourselves, except for the boundaries of societal roles.

Young people who experience divorce and separation in their homes use these experiences to trigger their inner mastery and to practice using those energies they normally would not have the opportunity to use for many years. Not having the parent to project upon, they begin to discover the essential core of father, mother, male, and female energies from a much purer state than when they simply take on the "hand-me-downs" of ancestral patterns. Children who grow up with only their mother, for example, have already mastered through multiincarnational experiences the exterior yang energy. As children find their way by using such powerful essence material, they will automatically alter for future generations the quality of the masculine expression. Because the child can express tenderness and vulnerability as well as the flexibility to surrender, the whole flavor of yang energy will be altered, much for the good of humanity.

Instead of supporting emotional confusion when a child loses one parent, we could better respect the decision made by the child's soul to have the experience for growth, as an expression of its own power.

If our father or mother dies, this implies a kind of initiation for us. The energy expressed and projected by the parent leaves its bearer and immediately belongs to the child. The child inherits and internalizes this energy and has the opportunity of merging with it to such an extent that he can radiate it himself.

If we are witness to a separation in a family, it makes more sense to help the child go forward and also express on a spiritual octave what he or she has already received, rather than assuming disadvantages and problems that deny the power of choice. If children and adolescents gain the insight that the separation represents an important chance for their own development, they will be able to combine and live the male and the female energies in a new way.

When partners separate, they experience the same anxieties and fears as the children. There follows an initiation for each of the partners, especially for the person who possibly does not want the divorce or separation. Just like the children, the adults have to experience something new within themselves; they have to assimilate forces they once projected onto the partner. There comes a period dominated by the fear of loneliness, of the imagined inability to find fulfillment and to deal with the demands made by life. However, through the challenge, the man discovers that he can learn how to cook and, even more crucial, how to nurture. The woman learns how to earn money and feed the family. If the partners formerly believed it impossible to survive each without the other, they now realize that they can deal with those things themselves that they used to leave to their partner.

The quickening of emotional initiations is inclusive of all souls today, no matter what their chronological age. All over the world children are dealing with emotional experiences that formerly only adults underwent. Children have love relationships, are plagued by identity crises, and have to cope with jealousy and fear because their emotional life is more intense. What seemingly used to be a prerogative of teenagers and young adults is now shared by eight- to ten-year-olds. Obviously this causes a great deal of confusion and anxiety. But to the degree that young people learn of their soul's teaching at an early age, they also become able to penetrate new dimensions of consciousness that offer the only real comfort within the funnel of initiation. Viewed from the spiritual perspective, the tests of living are always wonderful opportunities to get in touch with our true selves. The Higher Self never offers us an experience we cannot use, that we cannot translate into a gift. When we view our life experiences in this way, instead of considering ourselves as victims, we quickly and comprehensively awaken spiritually. We are given the choice to shape our lives creatively from a position of true power.

✐   *The Healing Flow of Energy*   ↘

The universe is filled with energy that can be plucked by us to assist our bodily experience. The sky, the water, the earth, everywhere we turn there is a source of radiant energy available for our use. Just the fact that there is motion creates a force that brings health. As long as there is movement, the flow of energy itself clears, replenishes, and heals everything in its path. It is when there is a static buildup that imbalance becomes threatening. The basis of Chinese medicine and several other ancient systems of healing is exactly this recognition of the universal laws of motion, whether the flow is that of fluid, gas, or even more solid particles of matter.

Move we must! No different from the body, not exempt from action and reaction, the pulse lives in us. The heart beats, birth to death, day to night. So, too, with feelings and thought, there must be change in order to grow. In relationships we suffer the misconception that only if we maintain status quo are we safe. This is just the incrustation of the emotional body. The reality is that only if we become fresh and new with every day will we live in truth together. Our growing gives impetus to all those in our karmic pool to grow, too. If one corner point of the triangle moves, the other points must also move to keep the equilibrium. This is the kiss, the gift, of life!

The goal is to no longer consider ourselves as rigid forms and structures. We are living bearers of energies, we are energetic systems, we are moving, fluid light. Every kind of multidimensional work exalts us to become involved with the unmanifest, to delight ourselves in opening up to it. This, in its turn, will change our perception of reality, as well as the reality itself. This universal flow of energy belongs to us, it is unlimited, and it will fill us with life. That very sense of fullness allows us to become exuberant givers, to become an important link in the chain, to experience that we belong.

A marvelous meditation is to open the vortex at the crown chakra, at the top of the head, and call in the universal flow of energy. Let us perceive that we are looking at the warm sun, letting it fill us with its powerful energy, feeling the warmth and the radiance with all our senses on our skin, in our cells, feeling how our face begins to glow, feeling illuminated and elated in such a way that we completely forget our body. This is a little exercise that anyone can easily do.

We have all certainly experienced at some time how we could forget our bodily structure. Connected with this forgetting is an inner elation, a relief, a floating sensation. Many of us have had out-of-body experiences and are therefore freed from the illusion that we are imprisoned here, in physical form. We most certainly are not. We can even choose our death, its form and time. Often in sessions at the Light Institute people describe in detail what took place after their death, what happened to the others in their life, and have lucid conscious perception of the energetic dimensions that were subsequently available to them.

Even when there are borders, such as the triangles of relationship or the limitations of physical form, if we align with the flow of energy, we can experience ourselves as the ecstatic spin, spiraling up, bursting out from the fountain of consciousness. Life is magical. Let us awaken the Fearless Self and truly, freely live it!

9

*Exercises
for
Consciousness*

✔ *Consciousness Alone Can Heal Emotions* ➤

The art of consciousness is attention. It is not an inherited skill, a faculty of only the intelligent ones, something that can be bought or sold. It is the essence of the soul that sleeps within the mind of the cell and permeates all our subtle bodies. Consciousness is, however, a discipline that requires surrender of the ego, a truce of the emotional body. Once this threshold is passed, it comes to us easily, although in increments like the waves on the shore of the incoming tide.

Initially the emotional body resists conscious expansion because it is like the guilty child being discovered by the parent who thwarts its play. If it is engaged in projection of blame or responsibility, or judgment and self-righteousness, it must relinquish all these cloaking devises in the light of truth. Once the emotional body discovers that it can express itself in new and delicious ways, it quickly surrenders to the sensations of elation and joy that flood it in the presence of the Higher Self.

Only the spiritual body heals the emotions, not the mind, which limits itself to the accounting of the ego. The mind says why something is true, or good, but it never makes it so through experience, which is our ultimate measure of truth. The spiritual body is not acquired, but it must be uncovered, as it were, because it is buried in the unarticulated reaches of our childhood, where its pure essence is encapsulated. Spiritual enlightenment is a worthy endeavor of the mind that can finally wrap itself around something that has true substance, endless requisite variety, that can bring it out of the shadows and into the light of awareness. Although too many people and religions have attempted to imprison the spirit within the doctrine of the mind, it simply cannot be done because the soul belongs to the infinite universe of radiance. It can be reflected, refracted, and embraced, but it cannot be limited, cornered, or owned.

On our journey to enlightenment, we can use the mind to heighten the awareness of perception. Perception is the great tool of consciousness within the hologram of human experience. We can begin our attunement to spiritual octaves through enhancement of perceiving the infinite web, the matrix of essence, of what is there. To this end we can begin to exercise perception so as to give ourselves space within the octaves of awareness that grant us peace and fulfillment. Thus the emotional body is transcended and transmuted without force, but with a kind of grace most of us never imagined we could receive.

We heal the emotional body as we focus our attention on the highest octaves and vibrations of our emotions. We develop the capacity to experience happiness, ecstasy, and tranquillity to the degree to which we can free ourselves from the residue of our emotional body. When the heart is filled with joy, the emotions soar. The purpose is to recognize and experience the universal energies of our own being.

In this chapter I will suggest a number of exercises; however, an exercise is never an end in itself. The goal is to awaken consciousness. At best, techniques can help get our consciousness in gear. Our Higher Self is already in existence and in touch with us, directly or indirectly. We are, in truth, light and divine consciousness. There is nothing that has to be created, we are simply not aware of it yet.

If we go beyond or deeper into ourselves, perhaps with the help of one of these exercises, we will discover new aspects of life. It is not a matter of discarding emotions but rather of letting them be permeated by higher vibrations and light-filled energy. Exercises can help us orient our inner spiritual focus to develop the energies that flow to the desired goal. It is more important to create an energy spiral or an energy pattern than to set up specific exercise routines. It is the consciousness that supports it that does so. Exercises are like impulses to focus on higher cosmic vibrations. If, for instance, we wish to alter and improve our relationships with our parents or partners because communication between us has become icebound, our actual goal is to change in *our* consciousness, not theirs—our goal is to witness the relationship from the spiritual perspective.

Exercises can help us to declog energy and overcome the blocks in our own consciousness. As a rule we are not yet accustomed to altering the vibrations of consciousness spontaneously and immediately, but we are all capable of doing so. The instant we switch our attention to conscious awareness, old games of polarity collapse because we don't need them if we can perceive, for example, that our honorable opponent is our divine friend. We play our respective roles in our life dramas without realizing that we can experience direct and immediate changes from spiritual dimensions. We can let everything run according to karmic principles in our relationships, or we can merge on a higher octave so that the quality of energy exchange between us is of a spiritual nature and not just karmic role playing.

Exercises help us open to new dimensions to receive new energies. Each new energy flow releases old residue and crystallizations and sets us free. If we influence it through focusing on spiritual octaves, the emotional body increases its own vibration so that residues such as fear, anger, self-righteousness, and so forth are disintegrated. Our sessions at the Light Institute are concerned with energies also, through multidimensional exploration.

I always warn people against attempting multiincarnational work on their own. Without an experienced guide, the trickster and possessive qualities of the emotional body may come to the fore and overwhelm us. We need a neutral witness who knows how to guide us through the sticky astral frequencies and into the light. The profound clearing process of our emotional body takes place on a much deeper level of consciousness than occurs by exercise or meditation alone. This does not, though, diminish the usefulness of the exercises. These exercises do not make us see and experience what specific themes and contracts connect us with other people, but they focus our inner being, which is a prerequisite to a peaceful, balanced life.

Spiritual exercise is a wonderful form of communication between the self and the outside world. We can do these exercises together in groups to heighten the experience of each one and offer support and courage in integrating our spiritual essence into our daily lives. If only one individual in the whole group experiences ecstasy, if only one individual dissolves an emotional block, the energy released also affects the others in the group, consciously or unconsciously. It is now time for us to learn how to use our inner creative energy without dominating or manipulating others, but solely to open up new dimensions of consciousness.

✔   *An Exercise with Light*   ➤

We can often observe people crossing their arms in front of their stomachs or bending over slightly in that area, even when they are standing. This posture is an attempt at self-protection because this stomach or solar plexus area is the seat of the emotional body. Via our solar plexus, we unconsciously receive the emotional vibrations of others. Normally we stretch out the feelers or antennae of our emotional body so as to come into contact with the energies of our surroundings through these delicate threads or fibers and to exchange energies. However, the vulnerable energy of infants and small children is confronted again and again with negative vibrations so that these fibers begin to retract at the first sign of emotional negativity. We all know the feeling of nausea or butterflies in our stomach when we are about to enter or are in an emotionally oppressive situation and our sympathetic nervous system is registering fear via the solar plexus ganglion.

We try to protect ourselves by covering and contracting the solar plexus. Unfortunately constant contraction of this area serves to weaken it, leaving us very permeable to outside energies. We can cleanse our emotional body fibers by extending our energy out through the solar plexus. This protects us from energies we might otherwise take in. As we do this we are able to alter the messages we are sending out to the world about who we are, and at the same time we can actually enhance ourselves through the higher vibrations caused by radiance.

The following exercise teaches us how to do this. You can do it anywhere, in the car, at a desk, lying on a bed. Just be sure to uncross your arms and legs. It is useful to loosen your belt or any tight clothing so that you are really relaxed.

Through your crown chakra, through your scalp, let clear, white light flow into yourself. If you think you cannot do that without using your imagination, then by all means use it! Simply imagine that white light is flowing into your head from above. Then let it flow out again through your stomach and solar plexus in the form of a ray of white light. The process is to "inhale" white light through your head and "exhale" it through your solar plexus. Doing it with your breath is an excellent way to learn it.

Lay your hand lightly over the stomach area to focus your attention on what you perceive with your senses. You may feel warmth, or an itching, or a light vibrating motion, or even a light electric current.

Once you begin to sense the energy, hold your hand a little bit away from the stomach, maybe two to four inches. Continue the process of directing the flow of white light, in through your head and out through your solar plexus. With your hand held in front of your stomach, you can sense changes and fluctuations in the energy as you extend your hand. Does it appear differently, less or more strong?

Gradually increase the space between the stomach and hand until your hand is at arm's length from the solar plexus. At the same time, take note of how you feel. Do you feel differently, perhaps better, more secure and open, freer? I hope so.

For the next stage of this exercise, continue to receive and transmit the white light without holding your hand in front of you. Now try to direct the "ray of energy" at an object. This could be a doorknob, a book, a chair, the telephone, anything at all. Practice this until you can perceive when the ray of energy reaches the object. It will bounce back slightly when it hits an inanimate object.

The purpose of the whole exercise is to understand that, while you are sending out light and energy, you cannot receive or absorb anything through the solar plexus. This is the best protection from unwanted influences. After doing this exercise, people feel, sometimes for the first time, how a harmonious energy flows through them to connect with the world.

You can learn to do this exercise instantaneously with a flick of your consciousness. It is perfect when you must engage in an unpleasant telephone call or if you have to talk with another person about a delicate subject. Any time you need to influence someone, this will make an important difference because energy transmission is recognized by us all, albeit unconsciously.

✔   ***Working with Colors***   ✔

Color is the simplest, most universal language of the cosmos. Color is light, and each color has a particular wavelength of light that influences the consciousness of cells impregnated with it. The beauty of this planet is that it is so filled with color and light. We are all very much influenced emotionally by these radiations. Color is a perfect tool for healing because it is so pure in itself, and the body's intelligence knows just how to use it. We need no special knowledge, no interpretation of symbols; we need not learn complicated techniques. As we work with colors we are dealing with universal cosmic vibrations, and all we have to do is ask the body which color it needs to bring about balance and harmony. We then supply the color with our pure consciousness and the body will effect the necessary changes.

If, for instance, you have not yet had contact with your Higher Self, but want to feel centered, there is a wonderfully simple way to do so.

Directing the question to yourself internally, simply ask which color you need to balance and come into your center. You can "inhale" the first color that you either see, feel, or hear in through your crown chakra. Feel the color flow in through the head and out through the solar plexus, experiencing yourself radiating that color.

As a result, the emotional body is penetrated by this color vibration, and you will feel its soothing, balancing energy immediately and directly. You might feel a tingling, a light electric vibration, warmth, or something similar. These are very normal sensations. The more you draw the color in to you, the more tranquil, whole, and healed you will feel.

A different way of applying this color exercise is to focus on people, places, and situations that need to be transmuted.

While holding the person, for example, in the mind's eye, ask them what color they need to come into balance or be well or whatever is the issue. It takes a little skill initially to not attempt to choose for them. It is crucial not to do this, but to wait until you feel the color choice coming to you. Then draw in that color through the top of the head and direct it to them through your solar plexus. Perceive where they take it into their body and continue to send the color until you feel the other person is so filled by it that she now radiates the color herself. Allow the color to surround her like a balloon or a large aura.

If you wish to release the person to a new level of relationship, or to be free to leave your daily reality, the following addendum will make that clear on a spiritual level. Ask your recipient to signal when she has received enough of the color to be released. Then focus on that person, lifting off gradually like a balloon, floating gently upward until she disappears from view.

In this way you have released the person and given her a gift of spiritual frequency that imprints the mind that you are each free to go on your own paths. We are not really losing someone when we free ourselves from our karmic ties to the person, thereby liberating both of us. Rather, what emerges is a new balance in the mutual energy flow, allowing us to recognize the essence of our relationship. Incidentally this little technique is also very useful when we have fought with someone or when we feel that someone has addressed us in an aggressive or reproachful manner. If we send them color, even while they are speaking to us, often there will be an abrupt change of behavior toward us. It is difficult to maintain an adversary position when someone is giving us loving support, whether or not we are conscious of it.

✔   *Higher Self Exercise*   ➤

People frequently ask me whether there is a special technique or method for getting in touch with one's Higher Self. The Higher Self is always present, always with us. It is not a question of method or technique, it is only a question of our conscious focusing. In fact, we are in constant touch with our Higher Self, we are merely unaware that the blessings and good fortune coming our way is due to the loving attention of our Higher Self. Even the hard times are a gift from the Higher Self, helping us to learn the lessons we were born to master.

Simply direct the request inward that the Higher Self may show itself to you in some way or another. Whatever shape, whatever color, object, or symbol it chooses, accept it as the aspect of your Higher Self that is at the present moment the most comprehensible or useful to your consciousness. You can really trust your first impulse here. Often there is confusion because we judge the first images not worthy, good, or overwhelming enough to be the true Higher Self. Thus the beautiful mountain appears and we pass it by, waiting for the formidable man in the robes. Yet the energy of the mountain might have helped us detach from human dependency, whereas the man in the robes would have, perhaps, continued a thought form that God is outside us, especially if we happen to be in a woman's body now. The first impulse that you receive as an answer to your inner request actually represents the Higher Self at this moment. Don't worry if you don't feel much. Remember that feelings are the outer crust of the emotional body. Your emotional body may long since have learned to filter out any hint of ecstasy or profound feelings that might get out of control. On the surface there is nothing very emotional about a blue triangle, but if you will focus

*on its vibration in the body, your Higher Self will go to work to transform
you.*

*Accept whatever form the Higher Self takes and draw it into the body.
Focus on where it enters the body. It might be anywhere, but it is significant
to find the point of entry and feel the energy of the Higher Self in that
area. Then mentally give the command to your cells to record this new
energy so that the quickening caused by the Higher Self merging into you
takes place. You don't need to think or do anything more, as the consciousness
has intended and recorded the energy; changes will begin to take place,
sometimes immediately.*

We must learn to trust the Higher Self. I recommend that, after
you have made contact with your Higher Self, you practice daily
having it take form and bringing it into your body. Making contact
with the Higher Self is not difficult, but creating a working relationship requires desire on your part. Get into the habit of asking
the Higher Self questions on a daily basis. At first be careful not
to ask questions about which you have a positionality, because
initially the emotional body will try to make sure that the ego is
still intact and in control. You will very soon learn to tell the
difference between their respective energies. Ask about which foods
you should eat, what you should wear, if you should go here or
go there. Soon you will find that the answers to questions you are
vaguely wondering about will begin to appear in wondrous ways.

✦ *The Spinning Exercise* ❧

Some people feel they have trouble shutting off the mind enough
to meditate or to tune into themselves. The spinning exercise is
a perfect help for this initial kind of blocking. Spinning causes the
two lobes of the brain, the right and the left hemispheres, to
vibrate synchronistically with each other. In our outer conscious
states, the two lobes pulse in countersync rhythms that create the
faster beta brain patterns of linear thought. This beta state keeps
us from developing holographic consciousness. In young children

and great meditation masters, the brain waves are in sync. When both sides of the brain begin to pulse in a synchronous vibration, we move into alpha and even slower into theta states that bridge the two hemispheres, thus making holographic perception possible. As the brain waves slow down into these octaves, the higher mind comes into play and we are available not only for inner knowledge, images, and subjective symbolic information, but also for rejuvenation and healing.

Normally we only experience such states unconsciously—for instance when we are asleep—but spinning can assist us to reach them consciously, at will. This spinning exercise is especially useful for people who are very tense, who suffer from stress, who do not meditate because they cannot calm down their emotions or thought patterns, or who do not get enough physical exercise. After spinning, the blood circulation improves, the body becomes looser and less tense, the brain feels washed, and we drop naturally into a peaceful, meditative state. The spinning exercise loosens up ego crystallizations and helps overcome the feeling of inner or outer separateness.

Of course, children have a natural tendency to spin around till they fall down laughing. They love the strong sensations of motion. Some traditional spiritual seekers use spinning to open themselves to higher realms of divine experience—the whirling dervishes, for instance. Every movement that makes us more fluid and supple helps us overcome rigid limits of consciousness.

You can let your own body consciousness decide whether to spin around to the right or to the left. Maybe you also feel like spinning in both directions. Spinning around to the left, counterclockwise, draws energy into the body. Spinning to the right, or clockwise, shakes off negative energies from the body. Our body possesses an electromagnetic field that attracts and stores electromagnetic impulses. When we spin around, a kind of centrifuge is created that is capable of prying loose extraneous energies. The turning motion is like an energy spiral. When we turn to the right, we move out old or slow energy and detach ourselves from it.

Just ask your body what is best for you to start, and proceed. In general, I think it is best to spin clockwise, at least to finish. You can spot an object in front of you to maintain your balance if you like. The Eastern masters suggest that it be done twenty-one times; however, you may have to work up to this. Then just sit down and breathe very deeply. If you feel any nausea, the breathing will alleviate it. Close your eyes, breathe, and feel a big, blank space filling you. This is excellent for communing with nature and the Higher Self, as well as getting needed inspiration for problem solving.

Help for Children

More and more people are beginning to understand that they have a profound spiritual connection to their children. As we chose our parents, so do we choose each child. We agree to be the vehicle of passage, to let this child develop through us in this world, in this life, at this point in time and space. Children are reflections of the energies around them. They have not yet learned how to protect themselves against negative energies such as bitterness, rage, or fear, nor how to hide from them. Children live in the present, in the here and now. Often children fall ill because there is a disturbance or an imbalance in the field of energy around them. This explains why children so frequently get stomachaches.

When we work on a spiritual level to heal our children, we are also healing ourselves. At any time, you can do the color exercise by asking your child, in meditation, what color is needed to be balanced. This is a wonderful way to give love to another person. Children are such good receivers; they respond delightfully to these subtle energies. A child who is having difficulty with behavior will often go through a complete change.

I recommend going to the children when they are asleep and actually working on their auric fields to soothe them. This will help when there are nightmares or even prevent them.

Hold your hands two to four inches above the child's body and then stroke the aura from head to toe, stroking quietly in long strokes. With these soft,

flowing movements, you are harmonizing the field of energy surrounding
the child and clearing the emotional channels of all confusion, stress, and
separation.

If we, as parents, can support this harmonizing of the child's
aura, it is the expression of something very powerful. It is a clear
indication that we accept our responsibility as parents and permit
our love to express itself concretely. This gives us a feeling of
ecstasy since it means that we can give, since something important
depends on us. Of course, this clarifying, cleansing, and calming
of the aura can also be applied to grown-ups; and if the other
partner is willing, it need not be when he or she is asleep. Since
we first emitted energy through our navel center and created this
energy through and in us, we do not receive any "negative" vibrations doing this kind of work on the aura. It is very healing—
for anger, for fear, in a love relationship, in the family—if we can
give each other such a present as a harmonizing of the aura apart
from direct loving body contact and/or eroticism. Healing the
emotions is a process of consciousness that has an immediate and
direct effect if we permit it to. To heal is to love. To heal means
being clear, being conscious, being awake. There is some similarity
between this exercise and backtracking work. It is of little or no
importance what we call the field of energy surrounding the physical body—aura, astral body, field of energies. What is important,
though, is that we permit ourselves to become involved—even if
in the guise of a game involving creative fantasies—that we allow
ourselves and others to be healed. Even the vision of potential
healing can heal. Every impulse that enhances higher vibrations of
consciousness in us is healing.

In our time, in our society, there are a multitude of influences
that frighten us or cause anxiety in us. These energies that frighten
us are of an astral nature and are material. They have weight. They
stick to our body, especially to the emotional body, and sometimes
we even perceive this in a tingling sensation or mild electrical
shocks that we somehow try to get rid of. Since our lives have

become more and more removed from physical movement and labor, since we no longer move properly, these forms of energy continue to collect around us. For example, even such a simple thing as having lots of rugs in our homes develops positive ions, which inhibit our aura.

Thus we let ourselves be filled with diffuse energies to such an extent that we no longer know how to get rid of them in a controlled fashion. Then we scream at our children or beat them, or we are aggressive toward someone else who does not defend himself. Afterward we feel guilty, are frightened of ourselves, and try to rationalize why we behaved in such a way. This is a fairly widespread behavioral pattern. So this exercise, this stroking of the aura and harmonizing of it, permits us to solve those diffuse energies without becoming involved all over again in emotional vicious circles.

When we have been aggressive toward someone or tried to dominate someone, the emotional body registers it and reacts with fear, the cause of which cannot be perceived by the conscious mind. Harmonizing the aura as described above does not imply dominating the other, nor are we stroking our own aura or that of the other through our own emotional reactions.

✔   *The Figure Eight Exercise*   ❧

One exercise that is especially popular in my seminars is focusing on the natural vibration of finest matter and energies. The symbol for eternity, the horizontal eight, represents one of the fundamental movement of molecules and atoms. As long as this movement occurs without disturbance, there is "harmony." If, however, this "figure eight" movement is disturbed, the result is disharmony and even potential destruction.

Cancer, radioactive contamination, and AIDS have energy patterns that disrupt the natural harmonious vibration in our cells, which is, in turn, determined by the "figure eight" movement. We often think we are utterly powerless against this disruption and the ultimate destruction of cells. But in my opinion this is not so. One of various means to keep this disharmony from developing is the following exercise. (This does not imply that the exercise alone can heal any serious illnesses!) I have also found this exercise to be good for meditation and for opening up to other dimensions of consciousness.

To do the exercise, you can either sit, stand, or lie down. First of all, picture a light energy rising up from your rump along the spine, up the neck to the crown. Then imagine this "line" of light energy turning around at the crown, separating from the head, and executing a small "bow" above the head, so that a little circle or ellipse forms above your head; then let the light energy return to your crown, run down the center of your forehead, your face, your chest, along your stomach, down between the legs, along the perineum, and up again along the spine.

The name figure eight *exercise stems from the fact that we are ourselves in this figure eight that shows a large stomach circle, goes from between the legs to the head and down again, and a smaller head circle that is formed above our head.*

You can let this light energy flow faster or slower; you can feel it right next to your body or in some distance to it. You can also make it very small and take it into yourself.

There can be an accompanying vibrating sensation, a tingling, even a sensation of warmth. You should take care to be completely relaxed, to expect nothing specific, to force nothing.

Participants in the seminars have asserted almost unanimously that after the exercise they felt revitalized, felt more energy and clarity within themselves.

Something that starts out as an exercise that one prepares for and does expressly soon becomes a completely natural attitude of consciousness: energies flow, circle, pulsate, vibrate, in the rhythm of the eternal eight.

10

Becoming Whole

Exploring Multidimensionality

Our consciousness determines our perception, and likewise our perceptive faculties designate the limits of our consciousness. Therefore, if we aspire to become a new species, or better our lives by discovering new ways of living, we must diligently expand our consciousness.

How can we find new, wider reference systems for our life?

How can we experience the multidimensionality of our existence? The first step is as in the proverb, "Know thyself." We must begin by grasping who and what we are. We have to take on the responsibility for our own life—in every way. We can and must choose freely with whom to live and work, the health of our body, what feelings we have, what thoughts we develop, in what way we lift ourselves above everyday consciousness into spiritual dimensions. Some of the things that occur through expanded consciousness seem too fantastic to be true, but who could have imagined space travel, computers, atomic bombs, or laser rays one hundred or even eighty years ago?

Thus far in our search for ourselves, we have used methods making us dependent on others. We seek self-confirmation and identity through and in others. We use the outside world and our environment as a mirror. Now, however, we can and must begin breaking out of these habits, leaving them behind, and exploring on our own who and what we want to be. We are in the midst of a generously laid-out, timeless, divine game of synchronism, of simultaneous events and processes. We are dancing in a cosmic dance for which we can arrange the music as well as the chore-

ography. We are learning the laws of energy that will catapult us
into the next millennium.

The insight that we had from previous lifetimes, of how it would
be to inhabit the body of the other sex, can already free us
tremendously from our limited perspectives. And what would
happen if we assumed that our home is not the earth?

Some three-year-olds tell us, out of the blue, that they are on
a visit from another star. A child points at the starlit night sky
and says, "That's where I came from." Many people who work
on their consciousness at the Light Institute experience repertoires
and scenarios that reach far beyond terrestrial life and the human
form.

Not all extraterrestrial beings use "UFOs" or spaceships. Some
galactic societies have a highly developed technology. Others use
purely spiritual means. It is a thrilling experience to discover
that we can establish contact with other dimensions and be in
those dimensions ourselves. The opening of the heart is overpowering, the experience one of ecstasy. Those people who experience this also feel physical changes, more strength, more
energy, more light, more clarity. During the sessions, this change
is tangible in a shaking, a vibration, often a profusion of visible
light.

Today we are at the threshold of a critical mass through which
we can become catapulted to another octave of reality. This is the
reason we are experiencing such an influx of help from various
dimensions, why we can observe a worldwide expansion of consciousness. We are on the verge of an ascent to a higher reality
in the evolutionary spiral—an ascent that we hope will proceed
peacefully and harmoniously.

When people reestablish contact with extraterrestrial energies,
when they feel the spark or the seed of the universe within themselves, they radiate this and they develop a love for this plant Earth
and its forms of life. They understand that they themselves decided
to come here. This is not a form of punishment for them; they

do not feel as though they were imprisoned here. What they discover is the gifts they can give the world in order to live here even more fully and to effect lasting changes on earth. This kind of transformation of galactic energies into creative manifestations on earth begins with an emotional quickening.

Anxiety and fear dissolve. The healing of emotions is experienced consciously. They free themselves from obsessive, possessive energies. Gradually they let go of their ego. While doing so, they develop their empathetic faculties, but also a sense for the cosmic humor evident in the game of souls. They find out that they came here with goals and purpose, that their life has meaning.

From a certain perspective, we are all "extraterrestrial." We are all of intergalactic origin. This planet Earth has been fertilized more than once by genetic seeds of various extraterrestrial species—always at key moments of evolution. This is also the reason we are noticing today that contact with beings and forms of consciousness from other dimensions, be it through UFOs or other means, is so widespread. There is an immense flow of extraterrestrial communication impulse coming in. All qualities are contained in us, and we merely have to let them move naturally, without investing them with our patterns, our judgment, and prejudices. Consciousness is energy. Consciousness can develop only if energy processes really flow and are not blocked. For the emotional body's octave, it is best to neither hold nor force energies, but simply to let them flow, to become relaxed and tranquil inside, to know and feel that the flow continues and will not be the same tomorrow as it is today.

Having spent so much energy developing our personal ego, we are afraid to let go of our habits of self-identification. Yet we evolve by transmuting our existent forms into a new, greater consciousness filled by the pulse of the universe. We can be inspired by the example of the color white, which is made up of all the colors. By being encompassed in the white, the other colors have not disintegrated. They have not died. They do not disappear. They merge in such a way that something new is created. Let us be carried, penetrated, by the universal energy flushing away all fears and inner blocks and opening up our view of the unmanifest through which we can see all aspects of ourselves. The conscious fusion with, and in, the wonderful wholeness of divine energy makes us happier, more inspired, richer, more secure and supported, than remaining cut off from the divine energy by the limitations of the ego.

Color Consciousness

Working with colors has proven especially useful in the stimulation of consciousness. Color is a much more significant energy on earth than we have realized. Color contains certain frequencies that act according to physical laws and directly affect us. We know that the cooler colors such as the blues and greens create a relaxing atmosphere; that the reds and oranges are the fiery colors that stimulate body and psyche. We can feel the colors through all our chakric centers; through our solar plexus, through our heart, or through our crown chakra. (The heart energy is part of our miltidimensional energy, part of our Higher Self, while the solar plexus is part of our emotional, human existence.) We must clear our human self so that we can truly access our multidimensional energies.

The wonderful thing about working with colors is that they are effective even if we do not yet understand them. Our own energetic bodily system is a master of colors, so that even if we do not know why we choose a certain color, we can still feel it. We all recognize the energy of color vibrations.

If we ask the body what color it wants to heal or harmonize, it will tell us exactly what it needs. Too often we are tempted to pick the color because we know a certain color has a certain effect. For example, we think green would be nice to balance the throat, but the throat does not want green, it wants orange to help it expand and have more courage.

Just as in sending colors to people, we get into trouble if we start using the outer mind to control rather than just allowing the body. It is nevertheless fascinating to know the qualities of the different colors just to enjoy the wisdom of the body's selection.

Violet is the color of transmutation that dissolves negative energy.

Blue is the color of relationship and spirit. It leads us peacefully into the realms of the soul.

Green is in the middle of the color spectrum. It establishes a balance within the framework of colors. Green is the color of healing.

Yellow is the color of consciousness, the mind, and also the nervous system.

Orange lends courage and creative expansion. It is the color of the second chakra, the "who am I" that formulates our world.

Red is the power of action, energy to move us and give us life. It is also the color of anger.

Magenta is a high octave of red. It is the color of spiritual energy.

Turquoise is the color of protection.

Cobalt blue is energy from the cosmos.

Silver is a galactic frequency and also occurs in relationship to inner dimensions.

Gold creates the body of the material world. Thus we make a connection to the material universe's frequency when we meditate on golden light. Gold is the matrix of the universe. It is formed by supernovas.

White is the combination of all colors. White is an energy that does not express any definitive position. White does not perceive the concepts of positive or negative, or any separation or division. White represents a fusion on the highest octaves. This is the reason some people use white in order to enhance their energies, in order to fill their various bodies with higher vibrations.

Black is not a color. Energetically it absorbs colors. Groups whose main concern is power, such as the police, judicial system, religions, and cults use black in their clothing in order to convey a sense of authority, of having the power to rule and to command obedience from the other "members"—that is, from all other people. In big cities young people often wear black more than colors because the world is overwhelming and they attempt to convey the message that they are strong and are not to be taken advantage of. By the same token, wearing black shows the need to step back from the world to feel strong. I have noticed that most people who wear black feel insecure inside.

We are in the process of discovering new colors. More and more people are experiencing illuminated, sparkling colors during meditation, colors that open up access to new multidimensional realities. Some are translucent and components of several colors. Others are translucent or effervescent and represent definite extensions of our color spectrums.

✦ *Processes of Becoming Whole* ➤

The process of becoming whole is a simultaneous going out and a coming in. Impossible to describe, it begins with our choice that this is what we choose to do. Although some people put their every thought and effort toward "security," there is no such thing as stagnation in the universe. Energy flows incessantly, gives us impulses, propels us forward. It would be an illusion to believe or even so much as hope to stop growing one day, to no longer have to struggle or press against the barriers, to no longer have to develop.

By the same token, do you harbor the hope of one day having a revelation and of remaining forever in that state of enlightenment? This is no more than a comic notion. According to cosmic law, divine energy is in constant development. It becomes manifest in ever new forms and experiences. Again and again there are new octaves of higher truth, of greater dimensions. The harmony and the connection with the highest energies lies within us, not outside us. It would be erroneous to think that one could be denied the discovery of other dimensions because of externals such as physical stature, age, sex, race, or station in life. These are all excuses thought up by our emotional body. We often rationalize to ourselves, "If only my partner would meditate with me, all would be well." "If my family were also vegetarians, I would never again eat meat." Behind these thoughts are both insecurity and the desire for power over others. Insecurity because we are avoiding our own decisions as to how to shape our lives, desire for power because we want to impose our views, our insights, and our attitudes onto others.

Of course, most people will not submit to these impositions. We have already discussed how a partner often reacts in a negative way to the other partner attempting to focus on his or her spirituality. If he or she puts pressure on the other to do the same, how can one avoid provoking resistance?

How can we continue our attempts to grow without threatening others? By using the natural psychic and spiritual channels of communication that connect us with each other from the level of the heart. Instead of trying to convince our loved ones to do it our way, if we simply ask them on the inner levels what energies they need to become harmonious with us, and then give them these energies, miracles of transformation will occur in ways we could not have imagined. Color is a great way to do this—it is a wonderful equalizer that expands choice and the feeling of love without allowing the mind to become stuck in polarity.

The gift of consciousness is to learn to perceive energies and then to give ourselves permission to use these energies as a part of our normal vocabulary of communication with the world around us. As the color frequency passes through us, it quickens our vibration and nourishes and rewards us for giving. It is delight-

ful to send color to another person when so much is given
to us in the process. This imprint is exactly the message we
need on this planet, in that giving enhances meaning and abundance. It is so freeing to realize that giving does not imply
becoming depleted, that it actually means becoming stronger.
The one who gives, gains strength, enters into the great flow
of energies and becomes the gift! Sending the color desired by
someone in no way diminishes our consciousness, our bank account, our emotional richness. On the contrary, this experience
confers great joy on us at being able to give something. By giving
on the spiritual level, we can bypass the limitations of time and
space, making contact even if the other person is around the world
from us.

Here is a powerful demonstration of the use of color to free
us even from tragic events in our lives. It is an excellent example
of how time entraps us. Diana, a young woman of twenty-three,
came to see me after a terrible experience that had happened to
her over a year before. She came from a rather small midwestern
town, having grown up in one neighborhood with the same people
living next door all her life.

One weekend she came home to visit from college. She went
with her father and a friend next door to chat with Jean, the
elderly lady she had known all her life. When they went to the
back door, no one answered, so they just walked in, as always.
Rounding the corner into the living room, they were horrified by
the inconceivable sight of the woman lying half-naked on the floor,
stabbed numerous times. Diana is a very religious person who
spent the whole year since the death of her neighbor praying for
both the woman and her killer, who turned out to be the young
gardener Diana also knew. With all her heart she tried to free
herself from the anger she felt and also the recurring images that
kept coming up in her mind.

Diana is a very loving, sensitive girl who had never really experienced fear in her life. Over the last year she began to be
terrified of being alone. As her husband travels a lot, she started

having nightmares and sleeping with a knife under her pillow. A feeling of dirtiness and psychic malaise came over her body. This sense of dirtiness is a common response to shock that comes to many people who have suffered terrible experiences. They often stop wanting to be touched. This is especially true in cases where there has been physical abuse. I felt this same sense of dirtiness take away my sense of sparkling untouchability when that first baby died in my arms in El Salvador.

This is the session Diana and I did to bring her out of the haunting past and into a present reality in which she feels she can choose to create a positive environment without fear. It shows the multidimensional levels and how we can make time fluid with the use of color.

(Ask the killer to take the form he lives in your life now.)

Fog. It encases everything around me. It follows me wherever I go. Even familiar places seem unfamiliar. I can't get through.

(What color does he need to change form?)

Red. The fog turns into John. It's so negative. I can't relate to it. I've never felt like that before. It frightens me.

(Ask John to tell you something.)

"I'm filled with hate, for others and myself." "I've never been loved, haven't ever experienced it."

(Ask John's Higher Self to take form.)

I see a child of five or six, radiant and searching. The Higher Self touches his heart. A wave of light goes over him and cleanses him. He is a lot brighter and clearer now.

(Ask his Higher Self to give him a gift.)

A warm, comfortable coat that wraps him up in it and hugs him. It is a blanket of forgiveness and love. His face holds emotion. His eyes become beautiful and unmuddied.

(What gift does John need from you?)

He wants me to love him and touch him. I don't want to.

(Ask your Higher Self to take form.)

A stand of beautiful quaking aspens. They are so clean and untouched.

(Draw the aspens into you.)

They come into my hands and eyes.

I need to touch where I live, my mother and father's house, and where Jean used to live.

I need to touch everything: my family, especially my dad, my husband, all Jean's friends, her son and grandchildren. I want to touch her dog, her geraniums, her artwork, all the beautiful things she made.

I am touching her bedroom, my bedroom at Mom and Dad's house, all the evergreen trees that surround Jean's and my parents' houses, and the aspen trees on her patio as well as the pathway we cross to each other's houses.

I need to touch everything in my house, everything she came into contact with. Everything needs to be illuminated, John and his family.

I'm spinning. The fog is becoming illuminated and turns into droplets of light. The light touches the ground, the grasses, plants, and flowers. They all become fresher and I feel this clarity.

(Touch John in his blanket of forgiveness to release him.)

I touch his shoulders and forehead. I feel I am touching his soul. He is gone.

(Ask your Higher Self to give you a message.)

I can keep receiving from the Holy Spirit that light and keep touching and washing everything. I will transmute it and turn it into goodness. I don't have to stay in the fog. I can do it as often as I need to. I can illuminate those I love so they can feel my love and I can feel their love for me. I feel the love coming in through my head and out through my hands.

I don't need to be afraid.

(All you have to be is yourself—divine light—and give that to everyone you love.)

I feel I need to touch my mind, it aches. I want to open myself up so I can love my husband and my family.

Jesus wants that.

Diane is fast becoming her sparkling self again. What happened to her and countless others has pressed her to search for meaning on the level of the soul. As a result of this depth of awareness, compassion has conquered hate. The commitment to heal and transcend the darkness will help us all.

11

*Awakening
the
Fearless
Self*

Becoming the Parent and Source ➤

Enlightenment awaits our reuniting, our remerging with the Source. In body, this event is consummated by assimilating all the karmic lessons set forth by those we choose to parent us, and having absorbed, processed, and purified, we embrace them from the level of the soul. Releasing them from emotional and physical projection, we emerge as the parent ourselves. This is the tree of life, the ancestral inheritance that moves the force of evolution. The tender new generation must eventually itself become the tree, the Source.

All children know of this eventuality; they love to dress in the clothes of their parents, try out their postures, pretend their activities and roles. They shower their parents with pure love, acknowledgment, and devotion, until one day it stops. It stops because the parent has forgotten the divine purpose of the relationship and so has tarnished the pure love offered from the child by relating only through the channels of the physical, mental, and emotional bodies. Without awareness of the spiritual bond, the relationship is a ship lost at sea because all the other points of connection—physical, mental, and emotional—are referenced by the changing tides of personal karma, growth by separation. Only the spiritual bond can take us home to the point of knowing our own highest truth for which we search, unwittingly, throughout our lives.

The child is still linked to Source and therefore surrenders. This is not because of lack of power. On the contrary, the power is infinitely greater because the child still feels the murmur of the One, the all-encompassing yet personified force of the soul. We

parents instill the battle of polarity. The child is born to the mother
and so is initiated into the vocabulary of separation. With each
day of terrestrial experience, we yank the child farther and farther
away from the state of grace, without even a nuance of its existence,
until eventually, in order to survive here, the child forgets itself
and joins us in our unenlightened struggle—to find the self.

If we could acknowledge that we have divinely chosen our
children to help us along the only path there is, the path of
enlightenment, we would speak to them, relate to them in an
entirely different way. Unaware that our familial bond is the key
to our freedom, parent and child each begin to project resentment
and negativity upon the other as we feel the constrictions of motion
tighten around us. Just as in birth, the narrowing is only the
passageway to the next octave of expansion; if only we could
remember, we could enjoy the process. But the knowledge that
we can employ joy as an instrument for growth is still unexplored
on this planet.

As long as we do not reconcile ourselves with our parents, as
long as we are not able to recognize them spiritually, we will not
be able to experience new octaves of relationship with our lovers
or partners. As we discovered at the onset of this book, the initial
negative emotion in life comes from the separation or division
from the divine energy. We enter into the world with a sense of
isolation, accompanied by a closing down of access to the cosmic
flow. After having thus become separated from the cosmic flow,
we again separate, this time from our mother during birth; then
comes the separation from one's parents and so on in a seemingly
endless progression throughout our lives.

We attempt to compensate for this feeling of separation from
our source by redefining our identity, be it as a member of some
kind of group or club or as an adherent to some school of thought
or philosophy. The original experience of division from the cosmic
flow forms a universal thought that permeates our whole life. It
is in part responsible for the fact that we keep entering the vicious

cycle of reactions based on our emotional patterns. Every new identification with some larger entity is an attempt to regain our connection to the universal energies, to leave our isolation behind us.

We realize very early on that we are alone. We want to bridge this aloneness somehow and join up with something or someone. This usually leads to a false sense of security, which is bound to crumble sooner or later. In vain we try to find our center in the outside world, not realizing that our only source is the universe itself!

Expansion of our consciousness helps us view our parents as part of the group of souls closest to us. We not only share genetic patterns, we also have the same universal, spiritual traits. We are soul-mates who sought, found, and chose each other to play out our life plans in changing roles. The theme of the play is development of the soul. Young people as well as adults into their eighties become transformed when they release the bondage of mutual karma with their parents. As each being is set free, it creates an echo of "morphic resonance" that stirs into motion the lifting of karma for all other beings. Only then will true love develop among human beings.

When we speak of people connecting with one another, we do not mean that teenagers need to assume their parents' ideology. The parents' thought patterns will in any case sooner or later show themselves to be too constrictive for the children growing up in today's world, for these thought patterns have nothing to do with the essential connection of souls among the family members; they are merely instruments in the development of the emotional body. By acknowledging how important the role of the parents is to us, we can begin to rid ourselves of the idea that we will never be whole until we have divested ourselves of them completely. It is not their thoughts or life-styles that brought them to us. We can be different yet loving if we have the tools of consciousness to help us. True wholeness for humanity will always be inclusive of all our soul-mates, whether they be our parents, children, spouses, or lovers.

It is because we are still fighting for our identity that there is so much disharmony between men and women. Both are still caught up in a power struggle. The solution of the problem lies in feeling one's own divine energy and communicating with this same energy in the other person.

As we explore how we ourselves are responsible for everything that happens to us, our perspective of life and our way of living will change. Energies will be awakened in us that lead to healing and to creative activity. Just as there is a meaning to every individual life, there is also a collective meaning to life. There is a reason all of us have become incarnated at this time on this planet, why we are all confronted simultaneously by the threats of radioactivity, cancer, AIDS, and the like. That people are dying of hunger in Africa has something to do with us here. Death, no matter where on earth it occurs, concerns us all. As we become the Source, we will learn to merge our magnificent energies to meet the challenges of living together.

✎   *Planetary Survival*   *☙*

Survival is a topic of discussion around the entire planet, one that is often accompanied by fear. The fear begins with the feeling that we live in a world in which our energies can neither protect us nor be used to contribute. In spiritual dimensions our energies flow without abatement, but here we are suddenly subject to the constrictive laws of a physical reality. We are cloaked in low, slow vibrations. In this environment it is difficult to remember that thought forms can create abundance and that the universal hologram is always present.

From the moment we are born, survival becomes the predominant theme. Survival is a linear, either/or concept. "I can only survive if I subdue you. We cannot both have it, do it, be it." Suffering the illusion of the survival theme will always cause us to be worried about someone threatening or exploiting us emotionally, financially, or physically. Our vital energy is sucked away from the meaning and purpose of our life. Thus our concentration is distracted from our center and directed outward; we get more and more caught up in the vicious cycle of a self-nourishing fear.

We can never dissolve fear by looking to the outside world. We must give up the thought pattern, created by the yang energy, that self-assertion can take place only in opposition to others. This release of survival stress must happen on a direct, personal octave so that we can use the universal laws of manifestation in which we participate on a global scale. By focusing on the deep, revitalizing energy of the Higher Self, we can remember that we are safe in the womb of our eternal consciousness. We are universal beings, neither male nor female, young nor old—but whole. The meaning of life is to develop our spiritual reality on the soul level so that we become fearless enough to help the evolution of our species into a social superorganism, boundless and immortal. As it goes for us, so it goes for our friend and ally, planet Earth.

Emerging Fusion

If we become capable of experiencing our own center, we can also realize the spiritual design of an emerging fusion with all human beings. The polarity between man and woman challenges us to find a new wholeness by bringing together the opposing forces to create a fusion that will spark the world. We will grasp the hologram only if we flow back without resistance to the source of our being, to the origin of our reality. We can heal external separations and divisions by developing internal spiritual energies that alter outside reality. Divine combustion is the result of merging the yin and the yang, the seen and the unseen worlds.

We do not have to be different from others in order to assert our own existence. Although we do not have to assume their concepts and views, we need not reject them merely for the sake of our individuality. This does not imply that we should become identical with one another, it simply means that we must learn that every one of us is an echo of the whole.

By experiencing how we can dissolve the karmic contracts between ourselves and our soul-mates, we gain immense new freedom; we live the ecstasy of liberating new energies. We are truly free to merge with other people only if we are no longer bound in karmic constraints that lead to a reactive way of living. Once we release the fear of losing our individual persona, we will begin an adventure never before experienced by humanity: that of merging ourselves as one being. The Native Americans spoke of this oneness when describing meetings of consensus in which they would wait, even for days, "until there is only one heart."

It takes tremendous power and courage to surrender ourselves to a larger whole, but the reward is blissful completion.

We humans were made for this; we long to return to a distant memory we all carry deep inside. It is a memory of oneness, of home. Merging can take place when the energies are exactly matched. By learning about the laws of energy, we can choose to align our energies with *anyone* to bring about merging. It is easy and wondrous to discover our own energy patterns. When each being is whole and neither needs anything from the other, the frequencies are so compatible that they rush together to spark the fusion that radiates out and heals the world. This emerging fusion can take place not only between lovers and friends, but also between children and parents and with virtually anyone we choose to embrace on the soul level.

✄ *Nizhoni, the School for Global Consciousness* ➤

From the octave of intuition and creative power, many great insights, all profound truths and essential teachings that serve and uplift humanity, have emanated. From this domain, my Higher Self inspired me to found a school in order to meet with young people from all over the globe to form a synthesis whereby we might learn to heal the emotions, walk in beauty, and make the kind of effective, positive contributions that will re-create the earth.

We are a global family. Young people need to have the opportunity to participate consciously in the quality of life, the global truths we all share, and the choices that will bring forth the future. The purpose of the Nizhoni School for Global Consciousness is to assist adolescents to gain access to their Higher Selves and use this greatest of all guidance to create conscious choices on a spiritual octave, which will, in turn, manifest in their environments.

Nizhoni students comprehend that, in their still growing bodies they already are fully developed spiritual beings who have chosen to participate in global events during this critical period. At Nizhoni they will understand what their gift to the world is so that they can free themselves from the fear-inducing concepts that usually rule our lives.

In our Nizhoni School we help young people to discover their multidimensionality. They quickly come to see and experience that they can solve problems creatively, that they are here on the planet, not to be victims of catastrophes, but to be the solvers of them. Our experience in the Light Institute has shown that when young people establish contact with their Higher Self, not only do they gain more profound insight into their own situation and develop a renewed, more open, and joyful relationship with their family, but their family members are also freed to develop a new and better relationship with them and with each other, even if they themselves have not actively participated in the work at Nizhoni. This is a most enlightening example of the profound communal psychic of our human emotional body. In families where everyone has done the clearing emotional body work to release each other, the dynamics of daily living undergo a dynamic shift. Instead of the parent being the policeman of discipline, the Higher Self takes up the role of watchdog for behavior with infinitely more grace. Instead of the parent denying something the young person wants to do, for example, both parties can feel safe turning the decision over to the Higher Self. We have found that the young people treat this new power in a very sacred way and never violate it through manipulation, the mandate of the Higher Self. Once they have meditated on and asked their Higher Self whether they should do something or not, they feel powerful and free to go on their way. By re-creating a family group at Nizhoni, our students learn to express one of the highest purposes of living together in a family structure, which is to help one another in living on a divine octave, in touch with the creative Source.

Nizhoni teaches the development of healing powers, new forms of communication including telepathy, and the profound exploration of the self so as to completely heal the emotional body. We focus on the common basis of collective consciousness, on raising up concepts of survival, and on the immutable laws governing peaceful cohabitation with all of nature. By communing with nature, Nizhonis have learned to call the sun and the rain successfully and to stop the wind. They are learning to detect radiation and transmute it as well as other pollutive particles in the air.

Human potential and global responsibility are two major themes that give heart to the future. Nizhonis will forever be conscious of themselves as possessing souls that are ageless, talents that are limitless, and energies that can transform the world!

Transcendence of the Emotional Body: Awakening the Fearless Self

The emotional body is like a lonely, frightened child shut off in a bedroom by itself, longing to be embraced by the loving arms of the parent. The trauma of coming into body and diminishing the flow of the great, divine universe is so great that it turns itself back to feed on the memory bank of its cellular experiences in body, which it continually reproduces in order to assure itself that it still exists.

None of us escapes the workings of the emotional body. Caught in the bioenergetic systems of the physical and subtle bodies, we are prey to the whims of the emotional body that so desperately needs to be transmuted and released. Behind the masks of executives and kings, scholars and mothers, lies the fretful emotional body hoping to be recognized.

Like a prideful child, afraid of the pain of not being chosen, the emotional body would have us believe that we must be separate and alone in order to develop our personal power and to survive, since others might snatch all that we have away from us. It creates a world of illusion where we must always be fearful for our survival, always trying to avoid the bogeyman who might catch us or punish us for some guilty thing we can't quite remember doing. Thus fear and defensive anger become our constant companions. In this state of struggle for survival, we can never find the inner peace we need to merge with the love inside us and around us.

Angst is a lie put forth by the emotional body. It is no more than a pattern or imprint that came about when we separated from the divine energies. This fear of separation is then further enhanced by the process of birth and other, subsequent separations. After the separation from the whole, we seek our own new identity. The emotional body creates the illusion that we can find something outside of ourselves, which in truth can only be found within. It projects onto parents, lovers, and friends in a desperate attempt to find a mirror after which it can model itself. The emotional body identifies itself with its negative patterns from other lifetimes in such a way that it is no longer able to act and react openly.

But it is afraid that change means dissolving its patterns, dissolving the ego. The emotional body has forgotten its source, its wholeness, and so clings to what it can recognize through its experiential memory. Anxiety, rage, depression, and self-righteousness cause such a low vibration that the emotional body cannot conceive of itself as being higher or greater. Considered in this light, fear is one of the most powerful strategies on the part of the emotional body to maneuver us into that dramatic situation through its contractive, dividing, and resisting stance, where we have no choice but to execute the quantum leap. We build up the anxiety that accompanies individualization as an aid, forcing ourselves to overcome it again. In actuality, fear already contains the seed of its own destruction.

Fear is the complete and ultimate bogeyman that inspires us, tempts and seduces us, threatens us, and retains our attention on an octave of consciousness that keeps the spiritual energies from flowing. It is anxiety and fear that in the end drive us to open up to what we fear is nothingness, to leap into the seeming abyss or to fall into a dead faint. It is precisely from this space of nothingness, from this abyss that we think will extinguish us, that the unmanifest spiritual energy can gain strength and become manifest anew in us and through us. Only when fear and anxiety have driven us to the point where we believe no help is possible and where we lose all hope of a change does our emotional body become prepared to surrender to the energy spiral and to accept it without prejudice.

The spirit is the remedy. Only when we can experience life without rigid forms of expression and move beyond the various bodily limitations into subtle states of consciousness are we able to open up to the energetic vibrations that are delight, ecstasy, and love. Our times offer the first chance in human history to escape from the heavy grasp of the emotional body. We can and must transcend it. We can ride the waves of energy flows by using the technologies of consciousness described in this book to help us become aware and to experience that we always have a choice. For example, the energy of color, so simple and unique to this terrestrial home, can free us to redesign our world and our place in it.

One of the most wonderful ways to heal the emotions is to use the highest expressions of emotion, such as laughter, joy and the childlike abandon that allows us to feel the ease of surrendering, bending, changing. We are truly the most dramatic and amusing creatures on the planet, and our antics are quite hilarious when seen from the eyes of the detached observer. We need to play. Life is not so deadly, nor death so final!

So much of who we think we are is nothing more than habit or posturing. We have given ourselves too few models of great beings to practice greatness ourselves. We must learn to dare. All of humanity should do what we often did as children. We tried on all kinds of different clothes and hats in order to see ourselves in a different light, to express ourselves anew, to explore ourselves. This is exactly what actually happens in our multiincarnatons: we try on different perspectives, emotions, experiences, and bodies so that our souls can expand their capacity to participate in manifestation.

Truly creative spirits in all areas of art, science, politics, business, and medicine have always focused intuitively on the creative impulse and the entirety of their consciousness in order to become totally effective through the medium of their chosen art. Some musicians feel inspired by God. Scientists sometimes dream the solutions that they were unable to reach through a linear modality of thought.

We can allow our unlimited psychic spin points to connect us to a vast network of associative data that will bring us the answers we dare to ask. People pray, meditate, visualize looking through their akashic records, and so on. If we enter the hologram of the cosmic flow, we start to see, sense, or feel symbols and colors; we encounter energetic patterns that access our old thought patterns and rearrange them into new patterns; or we even create totally new and astonishing experiences and realizations.

The truth is that *we* are the answer, the experience, the truth! We are untouchable, indestructible, and even lovable. Our emotional bodies are ready for the journey home, hungry for the pleasure of a job well done. Let us give ourselves credit for having played the game with all our hearts, as if it were real. We were magnificently convincing, especially to ourselves. The reward is the merging with our Higher Self, the awakening of our blissful, radiant, and fearless self.

At any quiet moment, whisper to yourself that you are transcending who you are at this moment. Draw the beautiful white light into you and feel the radiance of your field expanding. Draw in the breath of life and, as you breathe, smile. *You* are the all-loving, all-knowing Higher Self.

Glossary of terms used frequently in the text

AKASHIC RECORDS—records of all linear time. To an individual, the records of his or her incarnations on Earth.

ALCHEMY—forcing of the will on matter.

ANGER—a defense response of the emotional body to cover fear.

ANXIETY—an imbalance of the emotional body produced by forgotten multiincarnational memories.

ASTRAL BODY—nonphysical body composed of our emotional and auric field that extends out from the physical plane.

ASTRAL DIMENSIONS—emotional body experience existing in simultaneous space with the physical states.

ASTRAL ENERGY—the veil that carries us from lifetime to lifetime, re-creating memories in the emotional body in each lifetime.

ATLANTIS—a continent that submerged over 50,000 years ago when its inhabitants began to misuse their advanced technological powers.

AURA—electromagnetic field that radiates from the physical body.

AURIC FIELD—vibrating light field around the body that displays the emotional, mental, and physical states.

BLISS—the energy of exhalation after experiencing rapture.

BLUEPRINT—the capsule or repertoire of consciousness that holds us in the third dimension.

BODY—vehicle for truth in the third dimension that echoes spirit.

CELIBACY—abstinence from sexual contact so that energy runs throughout the body, not outside it.

CELLULAR MEMORY—imprint of emotional body experiences in the body cells.

CHAKRA—an energy vortex in the body.

CHAKRIC SYSTEM—the seven energy centers of the physical body.

CHILD WITHIN—the being within, which shuts down sometimes during childhood and lies within, awaiting reconnection and awakening.

COLORS—(as we see them in the auric field)—messages from the emotions created by the length of vibrational frequency. Can be seen by those who can visualize vibration.

COMPASSION—expansion of the emotional body that creates the true merging with others.

CONCEPTION—the moment when the unmanifest takes form, the midpoint, the fission when the egg and sperm unite, which creates universes. The threshold to the unmanifest; the recognition that there is no separation; the center point of the figure eight.

CONSCIOUSNESS—holographic awareness that allows us knowing from all planes of existence.

CREATION—experiencing and assimilating life, and then reshaping it.

CROWN CHAKRA—the seventh chakra, which symbolizes enlightenment.

DEATH—a passage, a surrendering into our true self without encumberment.

DEMATERIALIZE—to pass matter from the manifest into the unmanifest.

DIVINE CIRCUITRY—the figure eight, the whole of the body energy that flows through the chakric system and the master glands. The energy itself is sexual energy.

DNA—cellular genetic coding.

ECSTASY—exploding creative force, which carries light when consciousness coalesces itself. The marriage of bliss and rapture. The sourcing, creative force of the universe, the Higher Self in action.

EGO—the computer that orchestrates the body. The confines of self-limitation that keeps us in the third dimension or reality. It is the structure that allows us to carry out karma.

EMOTION—the outward expression of the emotional body through feelings and bodily sensations.

EMOTIONAL BODY—the emotional vehicle of consciousness that is an entity and vibrates at a low frequency.

ENCRUSTATION—encapsulation of thought forms, prejudices, judgments.

ENLIGHTENMENTS—center of the multidimensional soul; to be able to reach out to other octaves and pull in our genius capacity.

EXPERIENCING—chasing the molecular structure of the body by going through something in a new way, such as past lives, which then translates right-brain perceptions into the third dimension.

FEAR—the emotion relating to anxiety about the perceived possibility of the destruction of self.

FEARLESS SELF—arises from contact with the soul and awareness of multidimensionality. This results in the knowledge that our essence is indestructible and, therefore, there is nothing to be afraid of.

FORM—the extension of God in the world; the reach of the divine into matter in order to experience itself.

FORMLESS, THE—the universal divine essence from which form springs.

GLOBAL BLUEPRINT—the plan of multitudes of souls to experience something that will wrench the planet through a needed experience.

GRACE—the energetic process of transmutation, transcendence, transformation. It is the process of anchoring the sky, of bringing the soul into the Earthly body.

HIGHER MIND—the capacity to see the hologram, to perceive the truth in an expanded way. It allows a person to cognate on a higher level, to work on a genius level, where both sides of the brain function in synchronicity. It is the genius level itself, the other 90 percent of the brain.

HIGHER SELF—the spiritual vehicle, the power that changes and awakens the emotional body. It is the megaphone of the soul.

HOLOGRAM—the overall organizing principle of form, the vision of the higher mind. It is the point when we recognize we are here right now and have also lived many lives.

HOLOGRAPHIC THOUGHT—the left and right brain pulsating in union.

IMPRINT—all the thought forms we have on a soul level, along with all the thought forms of the souls around us whom we have incarnated with.

INCARNATE—to take on the density of physical bodies.

INITIATION—the focusing of the intention on the divine and holding it for a long time.

INNER GUIDES—beings that relate to our inner experience at our own level of expertise.

INNER SELF—that part of ourselves that pushes from within, always motivating us to spin the hologram of our being to focus on precipitating those knowings of our Godliness.

INTEGRITY—impermeable encapsulation of self.

JUDGMENT—limitation of consciousness for the protection of the agenda of the emotional body.

KALEIDOSCOPE—a past-life exploration process of going through many lives quickly as you explore a key theme.

KARMA—the responsibilities we can fulfill in a lifetime that will free us from obligations from previous experiences.

KNOWING—living, experiencing, merging, being whole.

LETTING GO—expanding consciousness so that a person can move out of the constriction of the little self.

LEY LINES—the energy meridians of Earth.

LIGHT BODY—the highest octave of the physical body that exists in the etheric.

MANIFEST—to take form in the third dimension.

MANIFESTATION—using the harmonics of intention to create what we need.

MASTER GLANDS—the pineal and pituitary glands, which radiate huge spans of consciousness from us into the universe, drawing in energy and information to us. They are our higher-consciousness antennas.

MATERIALIZE—to bring matter into form.

MENTAL BODY—the linear modality of consciousness that seeks to understand reality through the rational, intellectual mind. It is controlled by the emotional body through the biochemistry of the physical body.

MIRRORING—experiencing one's self as reflected by others.

MULTIDIMENSIONALITY—a new brain frequency beyond linearity that allows us to tune into more than one dimension at once.

MULTIINCARNATIONAL EXPERIENCE—experience gathered in levels of consciousness and reality other than the conscious one.

OCTAVES—the harmonic principle of vibratory resonance in matter. Can be understood by means of the piano keyboard; such as, all the octaves of C vibrate when middle C is struck.

PALPATING—recognizing in an experiential way.

PAST LIVES—previous lifetimes that exist in the emotional body and cellular memory, and can be contacted as a way into the inner resources, the inner points of experience. Working with past lives is a method of contacting the multidimensionality in a linear format.

PERCEPTION—the latticework of reality.

PHYSICAL BODY—the organizing vehicle of consciousness that has existence in the third dimension or reality as we know it. It is impregnated with memories and knowledge of its actual matter.

POLARITY—the perfect complementary and symbiotic opposite, e.g., yin/yang, female/male.

POSITIONALITY—that which orchestrates our perception. What we perceive through the filter of our positionality is our repertoire, which is limited to what we allow in, according to the responses of the emotional body.

PRANA—the divine breath.

QUICKENING—the expansion of the emotional body out of its positionality so that the Higher Self can quicken vibration.

RADIANCE—energy resulting from the ecstatic spark which spreads itself out into the entire spectrum of manifest dimensions and out into the black void of the formless. It pervades all.

RAPTURE—heightened energy of consciousness of the emotional body.

RATIONALITY—the process of funneling information into a place that you think you can control. This promotes separation within our very selves.

REPTILIAN BRAIN—animalistic part of ourselves that warns us of danger, such as radiation or chemical poisoning in the environment.

RESISTANCE—a survival mechanism of the emotional body.

RITUAL—actions taken that are understood in a linear form and that take us into the astral dimension in order to gain energy.

SEDUCTION—the pull back into the old familiar ways.

SELF-RIGHTEOUSNESS—a guardian of the emotional body, along with anger and judgment.

SEXUALITY—the inherent quality of our Earth experience that merges us with enlightenment.

SHAKTI—divine energy that is rejuvenating and empowering.

SHAMAN—a person with supraordinary power resulting from an alignment not with his or her ego, but with the universal divine essence.

SOLAR PLEXUS CHAKRA—the area of our abdomen that is the seat of the emotional body.

SOUL—the individualized aspect of the universal divine essence.

SOUL-MATE—our complementary soul essence that accompanies us through many incarnations and helps our consciousness evolve.

SPIRIT—that which is on this side of the veil of manifestation, although it is nonphysical, and holds all the imprints of the emotional body. The energy that interfaces with the material realm.

SPIRITUAL BODY—the most elusive of the four bodies or vehicles of consciousness that come to us by oscillation, vibrational waves through the grace of the Higher Self.

SURRENDER—that which happens when we finally let go of positionality and just fall back into our real form.

SYNCHRONICITY OF EXPERIENCE—everything is related in some dimension or time.

THIRD DIMENSION—reality as we know and experience it; the manifest plane.

THIRD EYE—the nonphysical sight of consciousness.

TRANSMUTE—to create change by rebalancing negative energies into positive.

UNMANIFEST—the created and ever-spiraling enclosed loop of nothingness.

VEHICLE—an organizing field that creates action in the physical.

VEIL—the passage to multidimensionality.

VERTICAL ACCESS—our sexual energy moving through our bodies, moving up through the chakras, which connects us to the source.

VIBRATIONAL REPERTOIRE—the range of vibrations from the lower frequencies of emotions such as fear and anger to the higher frequencies of ecstasy.

VICTIM/VICTIMIZER SYNDROME—the recurrent karmic cycle of cause and effect between the victimizer and the victim.

VORTICES—places on Earth that respond to galactic energy.

WINDOWS TO THE SKY—places in consciousness and in the physical body that can bring forth multidimensionality.

WONDERMENT—the state of being filled with wonder when we can embrace our divine selves.

YIN/YANG—the female/male or receptive/projective polarity of consciousness.

Information on seminars, lectures, and tapes
by Chris Griscom can be obtained from

The Light Institute of Galisteo
Rt. 3, Box 50
Galisteo, NM 87540
505-983-1975